WAY TO
EMMAUS

WAY TO
EMMAUS

One man's path to spiritual peace

Mark VanLeit

Way to Emmaus
One man's path to spiritual peace

Copyright © 2017 by Mark VanLeit

Book layout and cover design by Jera Publishing

ISBN: 978-0-692-87553-7

Contents

Prologue

Do you feel the desire to strike out on a quest, sensing some hidden but holy truth just beyond your grasp? Do you burn to begin your journey, knowing nothing more than that there is something you must do, perhaps very tough, maybe nearly impossible, to reach a faraway place of beauty and profound peace? Dear friend, do not say this desire is wrongly placed!

As for me, I have spent this long life of mine walking this journey of inquiry, seeking here and trying there in ways both ridiculous and profound. I know what it means to quest.

First, there is something most sobering I must tell you. I am a fool. Always when I have chosen a path from my own thinking, one that appears logical, challenging or even just exciting, I have utterly failed. After all these years and adventures questing for holy truth, I can offer you only a little in the way of profound words which might point out some clear path to the authentic.

This I can do. I can tell you the story of a life lived. Nothing more. It is quite mundane. And there is much foolishness in it! I can summarize it for you. When I was young, my heart's desire was like yours. And so I struck out into the world, seeking to follow the paths I had chosen.

But, all of them, every one, led to blank walls! All these plans and desires ended in utter meaninglessness! Finally, there was nothing left to do but despair, to give up and admit my complete blindness as to who I was, where I had been, where I was going. And it was only then that there was any progress at all. How can anyone understand his way?

It reminds me of a story. One typically bright, hot morning when I was a Buddhist monk, I came to the end of the long alms round. I had exited the fenced monastery grounds and surrounded by hundreds of burgeoning Thai rice fields, I walked a few miles to the nearest village. There I silently proffered my empty steel bowl to the waiting villagers.

When my preset course was complete, I returned to the solitude and silence of the monastery. My bare feet were sore and my bowl heavy with rice. I tiredly walked down the cool cement road that entered the monastery grounds. Along this road was a high barbed wire fence separating the road from the nun's quarters.

Tangled in a barb of this fence was a little flying squirrel. As we few monks silently approached, the small nocturnal animal frantically twisted, alone in the bright sun, trying with hope to spring away from the menace of approaching animals. But he was totally at our mercy. If we had desired his death, it would have been the end for him. But of course, we intended no harm. For the moment, such things were not in us.

As usual, an elderly rice farmer walked with us to help carry the gifts of the villagers. Above his wrapped lower garment, called a sabong, he wore an ancient, tattered shirt. Now the man stopped by the squirrel, removed his worn shirt and wrapped it around his hand and arm. Swiftly yet carefully, he grabbed the squirrel by its back. He began to slowly untangle the squirrel's skin flap from the metal of the wire, for the part of its little body that usually allowed it to silently soar through the tropical night was the very part that held it captive.

The terrified squirrel sunk its teeth again and again into the cloth of the farmer's shirt, battling for life. Finally, the farmer succeeded in untangling the torn flap of skin, and lifting the little animal over his head, he gently pressed its little belly against the trunk of a nearby tree.

At first, the squirrel did not respond. Shocked and frightened beyond any instinct or reason, it lay motionless. It seemed to have given up. It was now ready to die. But finally, after the farmer had firmly pressed the little animal onto the tree surface five or six times, the squirrel responded. Grabbing the trunk, the little being's hope in life slowly returned. The farmer let go, and after ten seconds or so, the little one leaped into action, scurrying up the tree trunk into the jungle foliage above.

So too for me, there came a time filled with despair. Expecting to die, I gave up. There I came to a place of peace, a place of rest before a precious presence. Somehow, someone other than I had chosen me for this. I had done almost nothing to arrive there. I did nothing to deserve anything like this. Now I believe it cannot be otherwise.

The truth is there was never any need to go anywhere. What I sought racing about was right here. It stayed wherever I was. All I ever needed to do was stop, look over my shoulder and acknowledge Presence.

But then again, no, what I have said is wrong. It *was* necessary to follow this long, wandering path all over the face of the earth to get to here. You see, I had to be ready to pay the price. The final cost was a death, in a sense. It was nothing less than simply everything. I sit here wondering even now as I write, am I ready for its full price?

Tears run down my face: I want so much for you to understand, but how can I pass on to you what has happened!

Here is another story, this one from the Bible. Just three days after the terrible, violent death of their leader, Cleopas and his friend walk back to their home in Emmaus from Jerusalem. Making sense of what had happened to their leader Jesus seems impossible. Their hopes for a new dawn of the spirit in their homeland and among their people now seem futile. They had pinned everything on this amazing healer and profound teacher. Now brutally humiliated, Jesus' life had ended in a grisly, seemingly meaningless way.

So they walk and talk, filled with their story of these events. A man comes along. He's walking in their direction. He strikes up a conversation. Amazingly, he seems to know nothing about the events that so depress and confuse the two travelers. They tell him what has happened, finishing with that morning's news that

the Teacher's body has disappeared and that some women claimed that an angel has told them that the teacher is alive!

Taking all this in, the stranger is unfazed! As they walk together, he confidently explains how all that has taken place is as it should be, that it is preordained, that every little facet of the recent events in Jerusalem is in accordance with the writings of the ancient prophets of Jewish scripture! He refers to Psalm 41 in describing how Jesus was to be betrayed and explains how the exact details of his death were precisely described in Isaiah. He even shows how the teacher's last words have come from Psalm 22! To cap it all, the stranger quotes from Isaiah 53, brilliantly demonstrating that a profound victory has occurred in the world, not a humiliating defeat! As the three near Emmaus, the stranger explains that the Messiah has risen from the dead in a great triumph against the forces of evil!

The man's view of things is wonderfully topsy-turvy as if the greatest thing that had ever happened in the world has just occurred! As Cleopas and his friend enter their home village and approach their home, the stranger continues to walk on. But they press him to stay, inviting him in for a meal, and the stranger readily agrees. Soon, seated around their rough table, they are no longer strangers. Their new friend, luminous now, takes the bread in his hands, blesses it, breaks it and gives it to each of them in turn. Shocked, even dumbfounded, hope awakens in the hearts of Cleopas and his companion.

And like a flood, the truth overwhelms them. This man has never been a stranger. It is the Teacher; it is Jesus! Their confusion vanishes. And in that same instant, the Teacher vanishes! The travelers sit there stunned, silent, amidst floods of wonder.

The ancient covenants, written and given to their people on stone tablets, are replaced forever by a new covenant, one written in their hearts. They weep, for the Teacher is gone. His work finished. Theirs is just beginning.

Everything they had thought and understood and believed was in shambles. Now, forced to release their precious delusions, they are free to see the truth.

So much like this life right here and now, no?

Perhaps you are still interested in hearing more. Maybe you have a bit of time. If you wish, sit down, ease back, and I will tell you.

Lord, make me an instrument of your peace,
Where there is injury, let me sow pardon,
Where there is doubt, let me sow faith,
Where there is despair, let me give hope,
Where there is darkness, let me give light,
Where there is sadness, let me give joy.

O Divine Master, grant that
I may not try to be comforted but to comfort,
Not to be loved, but to love.
Because it is in giving that we receive,
It is in forgiving that we are forgiven
And it is in dying that we are born to eternal life.

St. Francis, <u>Francis</u>, Adrian House, p. 17

1

Foundations

Very long ago, when I was ready to be born, my sister Mary came up and hugged my Momma. The truth be told, she was not able to stretch her six-year-old arms around Momma's belly, swollen as it was with me inside. "Bring me a baby boy for my birthday!" she pleaded.

Momma did everything with high precision, and this was no exception. I arrived right on time for Mary's seventh birthday party. All these years since Mary still insists that she prophesied me into existence. And through these many thick and thin years, we've been close, Mary and me.

Of course, it goes back before that, before my face was even formed. There are sketchy, half-remembered stories passed down about my mother's family originally coming from Germany and some French Huguenots, and that they came to America to escape religious persecution. My father's family had an ancestor who worked in

Big Sister Mary

Mom, left, and a childhood friend

Mom's elementary school class

Grandpa August and
Grandma Emily Lorenz

a coal mine during the Civil War. But that's it. My family history recedes, and after a few generations back disappears.

While I was my Momma's special youngest, my Momma was *her* daddy's special youngest girl. I think she might have been spoiled a bit, as I was. She was painfully shy, bright and studious, in love with life and the Lord.

August, her daddy, worked in a steel mill. When she was fourteen, a steel I-beam struck him in the head. He became different, weak and confused, and he no longer worked at the mill after that. Only a few months later, August and Eleanor were kneeling together, crouched beneath the kitchen sink, repairing a leaky faucet. As momma passed him a wrench, August slumped to the floor, gone.

Her mother, Emilie, had worked for years as a servant in one of the big mansions on Lake Drive owned by one of the fabulously wealthy Milwaukee beer barons. After marriage, she left this work forever. August and Emilie had built a two-story house with a store into the front. Emilie and the girls, Isabelle and Eleanor, ran the little store, selling school supplies and penny candy to the kids attending the elementary, junior high and high school across the street.

Back of the Lorenz home   The chicken coup

This was the time of the great Depression, and the country's economic woes only echoed those of the grieving little family. The three fatherless kids and their fierce mother struggled on. The children, Al, Isabelle and my momma Eleanor, gardened in the backyard and ate dandelion soup and bought necessaries with the small money coming in from the candy store and renting out the upstairs.

Emilie drove and trained her children to be disciplined and obedient. Above all, they knew how to work hard. Amazingly, each of them finished high school, then college, and finally attained advanced degrees, Al, a Doctor of Theology and Isabelle, a Master's

Uncle Al Lorenz   Aunt Isabelle   Eleanor, graduating
from Teachers College

in Education from Columbia University. Eleanor came within a few credits of achieving a Master's in Education (as a reading specialist) from the University of Wisconsin.

I had little experience with Grandma Emilie, for we lived across town, and she died when I was ten. But I do remember one day in the 1950s when I was just five. I was visiting her by myself — there were just the two of us, a rarity. She came over to me, bent down and asked me what I wanted for dinner. How her smiling 85-year-old face crinkled into a thousand lines! I had never been asked that question before. I barely knew what to say. I finally blurted out "chicken!"

Grandma got her aluminum two-wheeled shopping cart out; and as I watched from the curtained window above the now empty candy store, she disappeared around the corner, slowly walking to the A & P. Half an hour later, she was back with an excellent chicken. I'll never forget that meal! That single, beautiful act of kindness is all I have of her now.

My daddy, Elmer, never got a chance to be the apple of his momma's eye. She died of tuberculosis when he was just two years old. Her husband, Henry, broken-hearted and wanting to forget, didn't feel up to raising the baby on his own, so he was passed on to his grandfather and life on a dusty farm in South Dakota. Here he lived a mostly loveless life, treated as second class by his dozen or so aunts and uncles. Single-minded hard work dominated his youth.

He was a gifted young man, and when he was sixteen, a gentleman from the Lutheran seminary in Thiensville, Wisconsin, came out to the field where he was working and offered him a full scholarship to high school, college, and seminary. Of course, my dad accepted, and eventually, he became a Lutheran minister. He met my mom through his roommate at seminary, her brother

Al. Dad was handsome, articulate and seemed to have a bright future. They married.

Things were tough for the new family. Father did not last very long in the various churches to which he was posted. He tended to alienate his congregations, seeking out points of difference with parishioners and then handing out his harsh judgments. Father was very strict about things like drinking and adultery, as well as praying with other non-congregants. He used the tool of removal from the body of the Church (excommunication) liberally for those parishioners who did not desist from their sinful ways. So things would go until finally he would be thrown out. So the family drifted from church to church. At one point before I was born, the family lived in a garage. Tensions began to grow between my proud father and my proud mother.

I came along as the youngest of five. Years later, mother gave me a little blue baby book, a gift to her from my god-parents, the Weichmans. She had but little time to write in it for there were many more important things to do, but she did write this single entry:

Mom and dad, Elmer and Eleanor's wedding; Al and Isabelle are to the right

Mark is a happy, smiley baby who loves his orange juice and his bath. He sleeps well, eats well and enjoys endless attention from his two brothers, two sisters, his mommy and his daddy. Mark has always been a healthy, happy, pretty child. He adjusts well to changes.

When I was two years old, our family moved from our home in Minneapolis to a new home in Milwaukee in. A single family had invited Dad to be their spiritual leader for twenty-five dollars per month. The size of his new congregation had shrunk to the point where he now took the call and moved our whole family to serve a single family.

My first memory was on this moving day. Momma brought me down some stairs in our new house to the basement. It was a place I had never seen before, a great, half-lit space, the only light coming from a dozen small, dusty windows tucked high up near the tangle of wooden beams forming the ceiling. The walls were gray, dirty cinder blocks.

She placed my tricycle down next to me and put me on it. I loved my trike. Trusting entirely in Momma, I rode into the gloomy half-light. Then there came a moment when I noticed Momma had left.

Halfway across the immense, underground room was a large black patch in the middle of the cement floor, perhaps where the old coal furnace had been. As I approached it in the deep gloom, I saw it as an enormous black pit. I screamed and sobbed, terrified of the blackness at the edge of this world!

I don't remember much about Dad, but I do remember that he made me memorize a great many Bible verses. I was about three when all this started. Each Saturday morning, I entered the inner sanctum — his study — and repeated them. If I did it impeccably, I could go out and play. The first one I memorized was "God is love." Another one that took me a long time to memorize was "Holy men of God spake as they were moved by the Holy Ghost." Psalm 23 stands out in my mind as a major project, and there were many more. These words formed the superstructure of my earliest years. They spoke of God, a concept completely outside my day to day world, but of utmost importance. What I learned from the actions and speech of my parents was something more straight-forward. God had immense power, but if I completely submitted to his will (as represented on earth by mother and father), He would protect and care for me.

Dad usually stayed in his study. He had a wall covered with bookcases filled with religious commentaries, concordances, and dictionaries. Dad struggled endlessly with these books, for he did not feel the grace that God offered. First and foremost, he was a seeker, wandering from ignorance to ignorance as so many do.

Although he tried, it was nearly impossible for him to hold down a job. While his employers saw him as a model employee and a hard worker, he had no desire for a secular career. He always gave higher priority to his church, which often paid almost nothing.

One time when I was still in a high chair, I refused to fold my hands at Sunday dinner. Dad became infuriated at my repeated refusals until finally

Arriving in Milwaukee: Connie, Mary, John and me

he took me into the bathroom and spanked me. My sisters tell me that this cycle repeated itself six times! They were terrified and never would have done such a thing themselves. Why couldn't I just submit? All I remember was my complete intransigence — despite my terror. Neither he nor anyone else for that matter broke my will. Only later was my spirit crushed.

Another time I came into Dad's study and walked up to him. He easily put his arm around me while I asked him, "Daddy, why do I have to obey you?" He tilted his head back so he could see me through the bottom of his bifocals and said in the mildest way, "Because I am your Father and Jesus teaches us that you should respect and obey your mother and father. Now run along." And I did.

Much of my time as a child was spent playing, often alone. Lincoln logs, tiny toy cars and trucks and vast, complex landscapes of rumpled carpets and overturned dining room chairs made comfortable little houses within which I crouched. Of course, they were complete with cars and planes and airfields and spaceports and factories and, of course, lots of smashups. This was the world of my early days.

Things did not go well with my mother and father. Shocking us all, they sometimes yelled at each other, although they worked hard to hide most of their discontent from us kids. Dad was a legalist and had a big temper. He even excommunicated my mother and oldest brother on his sixteenth birthday for praying with my grandma, who was from another synod of the Lutheran Church! Finally, things came to a head, and an irreconcilable rift opened between them.

My family in 1954: from left, Connie, John, David and Mary.
I'm the little guy in front.

One bright summer day, Dad hit my oldest brother with a big board with nails in it. Now things had gone too far. Mother heard what was happening and called the police. Later, we all sat at the curvy-legged Formica kitchen table eating a lunch of hot dogs and potato salad. The wall was a light blue, glowing in the midday brightness. I was five years old, confused and scared, hunkered down eating potato salad in the electric tension.

The doorbell rang. Two sheriff's deputies entered and showed Dad some papers. His face was bright red. They put a straight-jacket on him. He stared at mother with pursed lips. "You won't get away with this," was all he said. Then he was gone. He never came back. I was too young to attend the bitter divorce hearings, but finally, the judge decided that my father and mother should be apart.

Mom was to have full custody of us, five kids. Dad could visit on weekend afternoons.

He took my brother John and me out to play touch football and fishing enough for me to remember these times with a simple happiness. But he was basically out of my life, and I felt his loss keenly.

I see them standing at the formal gates of their colleges.
I see my father strolling out, May 1937, under the sand-
        stone arch.
I see my mother, a few light books under her arm, standing
        at the pillars.
They are about to graduate, get married.
They are kids: they are dumb.
All they know is that they are innocent.
They would never hurt anybody.
I want to go up to them and say,
"Stop. Don't do it. She's the wrong woman!
He's the wrong man! You are going to do things
You could not imagine you would ever do.
You are going to do bad things to children."
But I don't do it.
I want to live.
I take them up, like the male and the female dolls and
Bang them together at the hips like chips of flint,
As if to strike sparks from them.
And I say,
"Do whatever you are going to do,
And I will tell the story."

Sharon Olds

Mother changed during the years that followed the divorce. I understand now that money was very tight. For example, I was allowed a single bottle of 7-Up once a week, usually on Saturdays; but we never lacked for the basics of food, clothing, medical attention, (Mom's cousin was a doctor), or dental work.

Our newly fatherless family attended the Lutheran church just three blocks from our home. It was a bright spot in my young life, for the boy I was loved God very much. I told everyone I met about Jesus. I liked to meet the mailman, walking with him as he did his route, telling him about Jesus. I knew the church was the place where God lived. To my small eyes, it was a vast, beautiful, holy place.

There was a large bell tower in one front corner of the building. From our house, we could clearly hear the bells ringing us to church each Sunday morning. The bells, hidden far above, clanged their deep, sonorous tones. I imagined the great weight of the bells as they swung on their gimbals, pealing out their song to the world. Somehow, I knew God hid in these things.

Behind the altar at the other end of the sanctuary was a great opening in the wall framed by a finely worked gothic arch. I thought this window led into another world. Hidden lights lit the curved surface behind the frame. There, Jesus, painted in robes of blue and white, floated up into the air. He was ascending into heaven. His hands outstretched while his feet hung down beneath his robes. There were

Siloah Lutheran Church, my childhood church in Milwaukee

little nail holes in each arch. Clouds framed the folds of his robe, snowy white against the cobalt blue sky behind him. One hand, also with its little nail hole, was raised before him in the ancient symbol of benediction.

He looked down on me. His eyes were intensely powerful, yet they were very gentle, filled with compassion. I knew he loved me. I felt safe and warm. He was real. He took care of me. The way I understood it, my part of the deal was clear: I just had to be good and follow his commandments. This was the simple rule of my life. Up there behind the altar was a man, somehow also the Son of God. He ruled me. We had a deal.

I attended Sunday school faithfully. I was very proud of my Sunday school attendance pins. Over the years, the original circular pin grew a gold boundary of laurel leaves and then many rectangular pendants, each with a year printed in gold lettering. I was a *big-time* Sunday school attendee. I knew many Bible verses.

After Sunday school our Pastor Voss, a great barrel-chested German in voluminous black robes, thundered out sermons from the ornate gothic pulpit built into the front corner of the sanctuary. He pointed out all the ways that I was messing up. I, as well as most of the rest of the congregation, trembled with the guilty certainty of our damnation. What hideous sinners we were!

I waited anxiously for the end of this part of the sermon. About three quarters through, the tone of voice changed. The volume dropped, and he spoke soothingly about Jesus and grace. After all, we were saved because Jesus had suffered so terribly so long ago. Whew! Even so, that last part had so much less impact than the earlier indictments. I didn't get this part about grace very well at all. How could anyone as holy and pure as Jesus care about me?

Finally, the end of the service arrived. I often relished this moment. It was the most sacred part of the whole service. Pastor walked to the center of the platform directly in front of the altar and looked out over the congregation, sinners all. He smiled at us. Then he stretched out his arms as wide as they went. His gleaming white robes draped gracefully from his arms as he recited the ancient Mosaic benediction:

May the Lord bless you and keep you;
May the Lord make His face shine upon you,
And be gracious unto you;
May the Lord lift up his countenance upon you,
And give you peace.

In a grand sweeping gesture, he would make the sign of the cross in the air. I bowed my head and closed my eyes reverently during the moment of silence.

Then the sanctuary filled with thunderous sound as a Bach toccata and fugue pealed from the pipe organ. Mr. Meisner, our organist and feared choir director, could be seen bent over the massive keyboard, pounding away, lifting and dropping his feet and swaying back and forth. Some people began to speak over the cascading gush of music, but I sat entranced by the most perfect sounds I had ever heard. Often our family remained seated for some minutes, listening to what seemed to me to be God's voice direct to my heart. The sounds penetrated in as deep as they could go. Somehow, I knew none of this was about words.

Finally, we'd stand and patiently file out of the sanctuary. At the front foyer, the pastor solemnly shook my hand. And then, dazed and in some mysterious way glorified, I entered out into the world. Sunshine made the tiny sparkles of mica embedded in the cement of the wide front porch flash and sparkle like diamonds. The arching elm trees swayed in the wind far above. My eyes were overwhelmed by light. Rushes of joy shivered my body. I felt the simple joy of being alive fly out of my heart into a world renewed.

While I hid the knowledge of His awesome Presence deep in my heart, I never forgot it. If I were very careful, he would take care of everything. My world was myself, my family, my church.

2

Breaking

Things at home were not so beautiful. My mother was overwhelmed by what life presented her. She had seen her mother, Emilie, struggle on alone, so she understood any family was not complete without a husband and a father. Somehow, her family had scratched together a living to support her mother and her three children.

Those memories must have terrified Eleanor. Now she faced the same hardscrabble circumstances. There was one huge difference, however. Emilie did not have an education, and mother did. Because of that, she could teach and earn a healthy living. But with five children, a house and car, and regular weekly food bills, it would always be touch and go. Silently, the joy that characterized the early years of my relationship with mother ebbed away, replaced by gray duty, tense routine and ubiquitous depression.

Mother expected me to be well behaved, but I rarely could pull it off. Like any young pony full of life, I wanted to kick my heels and run in circles. I remember once I ran stark naked down the long front steps to the sidewalk, pelted down to a huge elm tree by the road, touched it and ran back up the stairs, all breathless and silly. Lutherans just didn't do that sort of thing!

I adored and trusted completely my brother John who was just 2 ½ years older than me. One time my mom and brother John were visiting Ms. Woppert, a lovely lady who had taken care of me for half days during kindergarten. In her basement was a huge, wall-mounted dart board. I had seen a similar board on the Ed Sullivan Show and proposed to my brother that we play circus. I would be the assistant who stood with arms and legs spread wide up against the dart board. John would use darts instead of Bowie knives. What fun! But the very first dart landed squarely in the middle of my forehead and stuck there! I went screaming upstairs, the dart bobbing as I ran, while John raced behind, rapidly proposing ways we could not tell mother about it. Always John was my best buddy.

Another time, brother John and I were playing baseball in the living room during the precious morning 15 minutes between mother's departure for work and the arrival of our school bus. We had a ball made of aluminum foil and used our stiff arms as bats. Everything was peachy until I hit a homer right into mother's bric-a-brac shelves. She had a delicate little set of "city mice and country mice" all nicely arranged, complete with parasols and pince nezs, that is, until my death star metal ball hurtled through them, breaking them into dozens of pieces. John, an expert car model maker, sprang into action, feverishly gluing the pieces together. It wasn't until Saturday morning that our transgression revealed itself when my eldest sister, Connie, dusted them with the vacuum cleaner and the precariously glued pieces sucked into its dust bag. We were silent as mother beat her.

Life was a set of drills. Every day, each of us had assigned duties after school. The boys set the table while the girls prepared the dinner. Dinner was just enough. Hot dogs (we called them wieners), liver, fish sticks and gluey pot pies were standard fare. Afterward, two cleared and put away leftovers while others washed, dried and put away cleaned dishes. Meanwhile, another was laying out bread slices slathered with Miracle Whip, as well as apples and a cookie for tomorrow's school lunches. On Saturday mornings, everyone had their cleaning job, vacuuming and dusting. There was no need to straighten things up or put them away. This had already been done on a minute by minute basis every hour of every day. As the youngest and just six or seven years old, my jobs were to dust the legs of the furniture and the elaborate oak grill under the dining room table, empty the wastebaskets and sweep the sidewalks outside. Visitors would compliment mother on how well behaved we were.

One of the few reliefs from this forced-march world were Dad's weekend visits. Several times a month, he would spend a Saturday afternoon with John and me. In the summer, we would go to Esterbrook Park and play touch football, go fishing on the pier for bullheads and blowfish, or go to bike races in Lincoln Park. In the winter we ice skated, watched amazing professional speed skating races, tobogganed down the big hills in the park, and went to free travelogue adventure lectures down at the YMCA. These were bright spots in our gray world.

Fun was not part of Mother's plan. Fear was. I learned this lesson slowly over time, as I had a naturally lively and rebellious spirit. Constant slapping, shouted commands and verbal attacks were just a part of everyday life. Worst were the spankings. Sometimes, they occurred ever day. Mother had something like a State Fair ping-pong paddle that she used. The drill was to lower one's pants and underwear and then to bend over. Squirming away from the intensity only brought on more strokes. The violence was routine, uncontrollable and inescapable. It ground me down with its regularity, the sheer dailiness of it.

Sometimes Mother would get lost in her rage and lose track of time while she was spanking me. The pain, so intense, would go on and on. I would feel the injustice of it, while at the same time feeling the neediness in my gut for her affection. One time, the physical tension became so extreme that I could not help myself and I broke the rules: I put my hands over my bare buttocks to protect them from the stick. My mother started screaming then. She ordered me to take my hands away and hit me harder and harder, on and on, lost in her rage.

Something hard to explain happened that day. A part of me lifted up away from the rest of me. A crack and then a split appeared in my heart. I howled like some lost animal. I coolly watched the animal howl, while I remained safe inside a gray, cloudy place once removed. Eventually, the spanking ended, but from that time on, after I was about seven years old, the internal rift remained.

After that, I became tense and fearful around others. I felt safe only when I was alone. I cultivated aloneness, but then, of course, I felt even lonelier. A negative feedback loop of need and self-condemnation amplified my distress. I reasoned that I deserved to be alone. Nobody loved me because nobody *could* love me. Moreover, I didn't deserve to be loved. I was unlovable, and it was my own fault.

I remember contemplating my situation through the usual gray fog and realizing the insight that my job was to simply survive long enough to grow up so I could leave home. I remember wondering whether it was possible to survive that long. Of course, suicide was not an option, for it meant an eternity of fire beyond death. Like my older brothers and sisters, I steeled myself to persevere until I could leave.

A new presence entered my life, a comforting, furry darkness. When overcome with terror, I would turn my face toward this darkness, like an infant burying his head in his mother's skirts. The darkness enveloped me like a soft black blanket. The night was alive. This was my new safe place, my protector, my refuge. Sweet oblivion grew tendrils around my heart. God's bright light, within which I had basked as a youngster, became distant and weak. Memories of a warm, loving God quietly withered away, replaced by a new goddess, Mother Night.

When I was nine, Mom had a nervous breakdown. I knew little about it, just that I could not stay at home for a while. I was shunted off to my Aunt Isabelle's house in Fox Point for the summer, an hour's drive away just a short distance from Lake Michigan. Her place had been grand once, but as the home in Charles Dickens's <u>Great Expectations</u>, the place was worn and stained. The living room was filled with cobwebs and carpets worn through to the fabric and big piles of newspapers covered the piano and whole areas around it. The ceiling in one bathroom had collapsed, filling the grand bathtub below.

Aunt Isabelle had a loveless marriage. Her husband, Erwin, left for his precision grinding factory shortly after 5 in the morning and would return in the evening, silently sitting for an hour on a bench wobbling in fatigue, before going off to bed. Loneliness tormented me. One afternoon, I took off all my clothes, climbed an ancient apple tree far in the back of the property, not far from an abandoned, junk-choked play house, and sat there for hours, not thinking anything at all.

By the time the school year arrived and I returned home, Mom seemed to me to be OK again. But our family was in a build-ing crisis. The dark pressure on all of us was enormous.

Our neighborhood was in crisis as well. These were times of great tension between the races in Milwaukee. The burgeoning black population, pressing north to find housing while filling newly available man-ufacturing jobs, pushed at the older edge of my all-white community. An affluent black

Fourth Grade, 1962

family would buy a house at a ridiculously high price on a certain block located at the edge of the white community. Soon all the other white people on that block put up their houses for sale, hoping to sell before the bottom dropped out of the market. Quickly the block was "taken over" by black buyers. This was called "block busting." Many of the homes sold cheaply as the whites fled. I didn't know about all of this at the time and had almost no contact with black people.

At choir practice that fall our choir director, Mr. Meisner finally got fed up with me pulling the ponytails of the girls in front of me and kicked me out of the choir. Filled with anger, I stood in the snow outside the church, uncertain as to what to do. I sullenly shattered several church spotlights by dropping snow on them, smug in the resulting dark, just waiting for the regular time to walk home. I was afraid, for I knew that Mom would "whale the tar" out of me once she heard about what had happened. I feverishly planned how I would hide it from her.

When it was the usual time for the choir to let out, I headed home. On the way home, a 14-year-old African-American boy approached me. He grabbed me and showed me his fist and threatened me with a pounding if I didn't do what he said. I was terrified and agreed to what he wanted. He moved me into an open garage down an alley near the church. It was very dark out.

I did everything that he forced me to do, but it was sexual stuff, things that I did not understand at all. Soon, I started talking to him as an older brother, and he began to befriend me. He walked me home, and I plied him with friendly questions about his life, collecting information about where he went to school and where he lived.

When he left me, I walked up the dark stairs to the house and as I faced the front door my cool broke and I began to cry. I told Mom and the police everything that happened and where the boy lived. The boy was quickly apprehended, and I identified him as he sat inside a police van half an hour later. Life quickly returned to normal, the incident was forgotten, internalized and sealed away.

But the incident unnerved Mom. She insisted that I never walk to choir practice again. I ended up being incredibly relieved that she had ordered this. Much better to be molested by a stranger than to admit to Mom that I had been kicked out of choir!

That next summer I was 10, and we had a unique adventure. We drove 650 miles south to Huntsville, Alabama. Mom had a friend who offered her a job teaching speed reading at an expensive private school there.

I got heat stroke. It rained harder than I had ever seen it rain before. It was a place of extremes. On our first weekend, we decided to drive around and see the sights. We first stopped at a gas station to fill up the car. A friendly man came up to our car and chatted with us. Soon we were all in his car getting a tour of the town and its surroundings. I thought we had an excellent day. What a nice man!

That next weekend we went camping with him. Later, I learned that Ted first molested my brother on that trip. One week later Ted proposed marriage to my Mom and the weekend after that they married! Mother had just turned 50; Ted was 25! How desperate she was for a husband and father! Not long after, he started coming to my bed when Mom wasn't around.

Ted was very troubled, alternating between quiet domesticity and screaming, violent rages. The molestations became a routine and went on for years. I began to

Ted and the family our first day together

On vacation in chilly Kentucky

feel a deep, lasting shame. I shared the guilt of what had happened. I had let it happen! I had given my dignity, my integrity away to Ted in exchange for his attentions. I felt indescribably dirty. These were stains that I knew could never come off my heart. I loathed myself for my weakness.

As the years went by, Ted became increasingly unstable. He had wild temper tantrums when anyone rejected his advances. One day, sick, I stayed home from school. I was in the seventh or eighth grade. Ted also decided to stay home. As soon as Mother was gone, he began making sexual advances. I had been studying Christ's word in my confirmation class, so I brought out my Catechism and quoted it to him. I said that this was wrong and that he must stop acting as he did towards me. He became enraged and attacked me. I ran to hide in the utility room.

He was a raging bull. I wedged myself between the washing machine and the door while he ran at the door from the outside, eventually crushing it with his shoulder. Each time he hit the door, it bounced open an inch or two, but he could not get in, despite his raging. Finally, he stopped. There was silence in the house for a few minutes. I was sobbing, undone, completely shattered. I heard him say, "Well that's it, your mother's home." Crying, I opened the door and ran to meet Mom.

But she wasn't there. Instead, Ted came up and punched me hard in the face. I began to bleed. Hysterical, bathrobe flying, I ran out of the house and down the street, screaming for help, back to that old familiar place, watching the howling as it all unfolded.

Ted was right behind me. He tackled me on the front lawn of an elderly lady who lived about four houses down from us. She was immediately at the door. I shouted and sobbed, "Help me!" Ted sternly said that this was a family matter and that she should stay out of it. He pulled me back home and now sobered, left me alone the rest of the day.

John and I resting on the beach. This is how I imagine Ted saw us all the time.

The next day, several people from the state came to the house. There had been a complaint. They were required by law to investigate the facts as to what had happened the previous day. They talked to my confused mother and Ted for some time. My mind was a blur. Finally, one leaned down and asked me whether I wanted to leave. I paused. Finally, I muttered "No" in a small voice. Where was I to go? And not just where: who was I without my parents? The state employees left. They never came back.

One day I wrote a story about what I understood was sex. I wanted to impress my friends with my worldly knowledge. I took it to school and passed it around to my buddies, amidst barely restrained giggles. My social studies teacher was suspicious enough to come to me and request that I give him the story. I had been so embarrassed and afraid of getting caught that I had already hidden it in a culvert outside the school grounds. I guiltily retrieved the story and gave it to him. A few hours later, it was off to the headmaster's office for me. Mr. Leach, a very dignified headmaster indeed, gently reproved me about bringing such a thing to school.

But the real punishment didn't start until after school. My mother was the principal of the elementary division at the school and worked in a separate building. I routinely came to her room after school. From there we usually drove home together. That day as I entered her room she was staring out the window. She remained silent as I greeted her. She would not even look at me.

I was terribly wounded by this — and afraid. Never had she been so angry that she would not immediately discipline me. When I was a child, she had beaten me many, many times, but in more recent years (since Ted's arrival) she had moved to just slapping me in the face. I found this very humiliating. But now I wanted her to punish me rather than to be so frozen. I felt like I didn't exist when she acted like this!

It went on like this for four days. I was numb with grief and remorse. Finally, I came to mother on a Saturday morning while she was washing dishes. I knew that I was really in for it, but I couldn't stand the silence anymore. I pleaded with her to forgive me and told her I was very, very sorry.

She froze, her face to the kitchen wall above the sink. Then she slowly turned to me. I was expecting her face to rage at me. But instead, her face was a mask of the starkest fear. She continued to be silent. At that moment, I knew she knew what was going on in the house, between Ted and my brother and me. Years later, I remember that day as marking her final abdication. We never talked about it.

But now I saw that she was afraid of me. She saw and on some level understood how I had been intensely sexualized. Standing before her, I imagined myself unrecognizable to her, stained beyond repair. If she openly recognized the terrible truth, that her husband was a runaway pedophile, there would be a cascade of horrifying events, both internal and external. It was a truth to be hidden at all costs.

I imagined her thoughts as she walked through the consequences. After the splashy arrest and conviction, there would be a divorce and need to leave town to avoid the scandal. She/we would lose her/our beautiful split-level home. She would lose her job and would probably never be able to match her professional standing again: stained by something that wasn't her fault and over which she had no control. So, I imagined, she balanced all this against the status quo — and remained silent.

It was a terrible choice. She chose to defend her personal world and her achievements. Her no-longer-so-innocent little boys just had to be the sacrifice. It was in the silence of that Saturday exchange in the kitchen that I gave up hope. My thirteen-year-old heart broke.

I felt so crazy during those days! What saved me was my studies. I had an excellent 7th-grade science teacher, Mr. Walker, who amazed me with his understanding of the world and taught me the power of my abilities. I read insatiably. We had contests at school as to who could read more books and then write reports on them, and I routinely won the top prize. I read books like Dostoevsky's <u>Crime and Punishment</u>, Michener's <u>Hawaii</u>, Verne's <u>Mysterious Island</u> and Heyerdahl's <u>Kon-Tiki</u>. My mother thought they were too big and that I could not understand them, but I did understand. They created new inner eyes for me as I traveled the planet, exploring.

At the same time, back in reality, my old childhood deal with God — that if I were good, He would be good to me — bore its sick fruit. It dawned on me that the horror of my life was God's plan for me. What kind of sick God was this? He hated me! I could not imagine any other reason for the circumstances of my life. He wanted to hunt me down. He was dooming me to a life of intense suffering, and that was just a small down payment for my depravity. The world pressed towards me, ready to attack and destroy me and crush me forever. The psychic pressure was enormous and just kept growing.

Another thought entered my mind as I completed my catechism classes and became "confirmed" in the faith. How could God be so evil? The thought was unthinkable. Maybe God wasn't evil—He just did not exist at all! His existence had been made up by cruel, manipulative, power-mad politicians many centuries ago. I didn't know why or how such a thing could be made up, but I spent many years thinking about it. I discovered that once one accepts the premises, there are lots of reasons why humans manufacture gods.

Ted became the church's scout master, but soon after the appointment, he was discharged for messing with the boys. Then he became suicidal. One day at work, he took an overdose of some pill; his stomach pumped, he survived. Next, he drove his fire-engine-red Austin Healey off a cliff up on Montesano Mountain near our house. He emerged from the wreckage with only scratches.

A few months later, he attacked mother as she was brushing her teeth in the bathroom. He came in the little room, locked the door and began to beat her. Her screams and the crunch of his blows galvanized my brother and me. Together we rushed the door, shattering it off its hinges. We rushed into the tiny room, physically lifted our stepfather and threw him into the bathtub. The animal was running free now. Enraged and vengeful, beyond everything, straddling him, I grabbed his throat and touched my fingers behind his windpipe. Ted was a big man, six foot two, 225 pounds, and he fought back. I vaguely noticed that his finger was inside my eye socket. Roars of rage flooded out of my mouth. And then it was over. We retreated to our rooms while the police talked him down.

My family, my faith, and my heart were in tatters. A short time later, I asked my pastor how it was possible that this Christian God could give me a logical brain and then insist that I not use it to understand Him. He curtly answered that I just had to believe. I saw his response as grossly insufficient. Years later, John told me of an overheard conversation between that pastor and Ted. He was talking to him intimately, curtly, in a way that the relationship should not have allowed. We wondered whether they had a secret relationship too.

It was the last straw. I left that church and never entered its doors again. This happened just a few months after the formal church ceremony confirming me in the faith. Now, having done my duty for Mom, having gone through the motions of being confirmed, I was through with it all. It was time to

Confirmation

spit the whole thing out. Religion was a bad joke. I began to consciously erase Christian beliefs from my mind.

At this same time, the second divorce began to take shape. The last time I saw Ted, he was screaming out of a sixth-floor window of the psych unit at the veteran's hospital in Birmingham. "These guys are crazy!" he shouted. "Get me out of here!" Mom, John and I just hunched our shoulders and hurried to the car. We tried not to look up. We didn't turn around. We drove away.

Mother was shattered, bleak and incommunicative, the family splintered in all directions. Brother David, sister Connie, and sister Mary were married, while John went off to college. Now it was just Mother and me. Overwhelming grief filled my heart. I lived in a terrible loneliness. Shattered and splintered, alone and abandoned, betrayed and bereft, the only way I could truthfully continue was to abandon back. So I abandoned myself. The Lord, if he ever had existed at all, was gone.

God was dead. I wished I was.

Sophomore in high school

Looking in the mirror, I would notice my wide, staring eyes, glassy with an undefinable fear. I had difficulty concentrating and experienced angry outbursts for no apparent reason. When I was alone, I often wept, sometimes uncontrollably. Recurring night-mares would bring the moments of terror and violence back, all in Technicolor. I felt out of control. Sometimes, even being near others was almost unendurable. As I unconsciously hyperventi-lated, I would watch my heart pounding, lifting the surface of my chest with each beat. I saw Ted as someone who I loved and now missed. I lived in a world of gray depression. Undeniably broken, I felt beyond repair.

Fierce Dawn Earth Stamp Dance

Silent, stooped, sagging below twisted sheet garrote,
Feet hanging, cell bars all around,
Meet another addict of Hell,
An acolyte of Mother Night.

Twentieth century, Oh finally free it is!
Loosed from antique Father God religion.
Even 200 million grotesque deaths
Cannot sate the new God Power.

Meanwhile, we survivors huddle in our
Little clearing of established truth.
Mostly we hunt for food while a
Privileged few argue about Beauty's shape.

Know this, my friend:
A single hundred year blink
Erases every relationship alive today!
All is gone!

Art may seal a few in amber,
But all are forever dust
At the death of this single star!

Locked in we are,
While life's pendulum swings in perfect 2/2 time:
Happiness — unhappiness,
Dominance — submission,
Wealth — poverty,
Education — ignorance,
Pleasure — pain,
Life — death.
The snappy tune goes on and on,
Tap our feet to its syncopated beat, we do!

Written while a monk

3

Mr. Natural

The summer after the divorce, Mom and I moved back to Milwaukee. Mom was a bombed-out wreck, barely able to hold it together enough to maintain her old job teaching second grade.

My life was reduced to a crucible of pain held together only by Mother's need for good appearances and family tradition. I was just my stepfather's prey, betrayed by my mother. I knew she knew what was going on, and did nothing to help my brother and me. And amidst all this predation, abandonment, and betrayal, I looked around to find that the rest of my family was gone, rebuilding their lives as adults far from home.

Worst for me were the private feelings I shared with no one. The kind father God of my early childhood was a forgotten memory. Now I was ruled by a shadowy, demonic torturer, eager to watch me twist and turn away from his ministrations, his tools of death, my memory. Regardless of my efforts to hide from this demon, I carried around the indelible mark of his sick intentions.

An intense state of aloneness and alienation grew around me. I was separated, an outcast. No one shared, nor could share, my experience. All I could do was numbly grasp at trying to understand the outside "normal" world and strive to fit in crudely. I knew that everyone saw my attempts as the lie they were. I was sure they knew I was making it up as I went along. Every day I felt that I was living a lie. Filled with physical tension, subject to panic attacks and always fearful, I tried desperately to "keep it together."

My relationship with Mother was cold and without a real connection. She regularly gave me roundhouse slaps, as if violence to my body was the only way we could communicate. I imagined that when she looked at me, she was reminded of the vile, depraved history we both survived. She wanted to push all that away from her. My presence made the trauma of our shared past all too real.

My oldest brother, Dave, eleven years older than I, married in 1964, and he and his new wife, Pat, soon had a son, Steve. In the same year, my oldest sister Connie, nine years older than I, married a man, also named Dave, and moved to Dallas. Sister Mary, seven years older than I, stayed in Alabama, marrying Al in 1967.

While Mom and I began to put our shattered lives together again in Milwaukee, John enrolled at Auburn University in southern Alabama, beginning his first of five years studying industrial engineering on a ROTC scholarship. During the summers, John returned to Milwaukee, working for our Uncle Erwin, owner of a precision grinding shop there. John and I had some contact then, but he lived with my uncle rather than at home with Mom and me. He was everything about being busy during those years, lost in work and the driving need to pay for his schooling.

It was just a few years later that he fell in love with his wife to be, Kathy. He and I drifted apart as his busy adult life and family formed 1500 miles away. It seemed that all my siblings could put the shattered pieces of their lives together again. All soon had mates by their side. Each, in turn, slipped away from the family, disappearing from my life.

Mom and I each lived in our own little hermetically sealed worlds. We were the family's wreckage. Mom was mute, usually angry and always isolating. She was more a roommate than a mother. It was a time of distant, remote control detachment. I was unwilling, apparently unable, to commit to anything positive or new.

My isolation meant there was no one to talk to about what had happened, and I was unable to put things together on my own to understand why I hurt so. Now they call what I experienced during those years post-traumatic stress syndrome. Emotional and physical reactions to nearly everything were exaggerated; now this is called hyper-vigilance. Almost anything could trigger periods of gray numbness, accompanied by a pounding heart and hyperventilation. Sometimes, I lay awake at night and watched my stomach jump as my heart pounded. I never seemed to get enough sleep. Even when I did, I tired quickly. Through a depressive fog, I remembered and re-experienced the violence and violations perpetrated by Ted against me, my brother and my mother.

I also was very paranoid. I felt safe only when I was alone, so I worked hard to avoid others. "Normal" people around me seemed distant. Their unconcerned, casual normalcy tormented me. The worst of it was that I knew that living in such ease was unattainable for me. I was sick with jealousy while terrified in any social situation where there were more than a few people in the group.

My school environment didn't help. Junior high had been a time of academic blossoming, culminating in being chosen as the top student of the year at graduation. I had won many school awards and thought of myself as academically successful. But high school in Milwaukee was entirely different.

Instead of being a part of a small group of interested and exciting students and adults, Washington High was a huge impersonal beehive of some 4000 students. The school was atomized into many subgroups. There were the tough Italians, the gang dominated Hispanics, the sports-obsessed Germans and a new group of dropout hippies. Placed in "superior ability" classes, I naturally migrated to the bright, idiosyncratic Jews in my classes. Some of them were truly zany, but they seemed non-judgmental to me. They seemed able to draw me out of my shell. They formed the nucleus of my friends during those years.

One day I borrowed my brother John's old Chevy. On the way home from where he lived, I pulled out to pass a long line of cars. Soon cars started whizzing by on the left, hitting the shoulder of the road to avoid a head-on collision with me. Finally, the car I was attempting to pass braked sharply and I pulled back into the right lane. It barely registered that I had come close to killing myself! I was profoundly numb.

I was obsessed with reading about the Holocaust. I thought that I too had just survived a type of holocaust. To me, the only difference was scale. I closely identified with the dead Jewish victims and the tattered and numb survivors. At the same time, I identified with my German ancestry. My relatives had fondly made me memorize little German phrases that reminded them of the old home. In typically confused patterns, I identified with the victims while at the same time connecting with the perpetrators.

Meanwhile, the country was going through a difficult cultural and political metamorphosis. Vietnam was becoming a fountain of national pain. Watching the news each night, I joined millions of other Americans watching ghastly images of violence as Walter Cronkite described the latest deaths in Vietnam. Each night he closed his report with the flat statement, "And that's the way it is..."

It seemed clear to me that it was wrong that we were in Vietnam. I readily believed the widespread conspiracy theories about how we got there. I remember one theory that I read about in a J. Crumb comic book. It showed a crude map indicating that the South China Sea had been divided up and claimed by multi-national oil companies. Steeped in paranoia, it made sense to me that hidden power-mongers were in control of the government and had perpetrated the war to further their greedy ends.

The environmental movement was also taking birth as the Environmental Protection Act passed in 1969. I attended the first Earth Day. While the black armband around my upper arm was in remembrance of our Vietnam dead, it also represented my grief over our death-dealing attitude towards the whole world.

It was a time of agonizing, seemingly endless suffering. But it is amazing how resilient our bodies and minds can be. Slowly, over time, I began to heal. Part of that healing was finding an angry voice through which I could speak my heart.

I formed a club at school called Earth Action and became its first president. We passed out broadsheets at local supermarkets listing detergents with high phosphate contents and showing them to be environmentally damaging.

We spent a lot of time during our meetings bemoaning the insensitivities of our culture to the needs of the environment. It seemed that comfort, convenience and the needs of immediate circles of family and friends were more important to most people than the sustainability of the planet. Earth was just a big goodie larder to them, always available for the next food raid.

My compatriots and I talked about the Earth in a different way: as a genuine mother of all life. My drifting religious zeal began to focus on Mother Earth as penultimate consciousness, complete and infinitely mysterious. I saw people as parasites like lice, crawling on the surface of the planet, damaging and destroying as they went. People were depraved — their much-vaunted civilization, a shabby, petty rape. Of course, other hippies like me and I were careful to note that we were different.

I remained an avid reader. Among the books I read in those years were early seminal environmental books like <u>Silent Spring</u> and <u>Desert Solitaire.</u> I saw the natural world as a sacred place that had been defiled by humans for many centuries. To me, Christianity stood indicted as the chief culprit and its product, civilization, had brought us far away from our natural roots as animals. Having recognized and seen through to the core of our country's spiritual dilemma, we saw ourselves as rising above the depravity.

I grew my hair long. I saw it as my "freak flag" flying high. I started using drugs, especially marijuana. My love of rock-and-roll music flourished. I listened to "our" music as loud as possible, making the plates in the kitchen cabinets on the other side of my bedroom wall shake and rattle. I adored the heavy bass lines and wild electric flourishes of Led Zeppelin and Jimi Hendrix. I brooded with Richie Havens, Crosby, Stills, Nash & Young, Pink Floyd, Joan Baez and Bob Dylan. Most of all I loved the Beatles, especially John Lennon's songs with their fiery anti-culture polemics.

In my first apartment after graduation

I was sure that somehow all we needed was love — and a rapier tongue to pop the pretensions of the previous generation. Here was my place to stand in the world. I became a spokesman for the moral high ground, the moral minority. I began to believe that through all this I was gaining a real voice of integrity. Finally, my life had meaning and direction.

I began to date girls. As a junior in high school, I fell in love with Sheila, a beautiful dancer with long, exquisite legs. She could kiss like the moon and stars! For two months, I was delirious with infatuation. Then she unceremoniously dumped me after she watched me follow close behind other mini-skirted students at school. I was devastated and for months afterward had difficulty rebounding.

Then there was Josie. She was a beautiful girl with a bright smile and long auburn hair. We met after a talk I gave at another high school, explaining how they could set up their own environmental action club. Josie was tender-hearted and an accomplished cellist, sitting second chair in the all-city orchestra. We grew close.

And then graduation! Such freedom! That summer my best friend, Ford, and I hitchhiked out west, and for the first time, I saw the immense, staggering beauty of the Rocky Mountains and the west coast. We spent time hiking in Glacier National Park and a single night at Waterton Park's magnificent Prince of Wales Hotel. One morning after sleeping on the forest floor a few hundred yards from Yellowstone's circle drive, I woke to see an enormous moose and her child towering above me, walking by just a few feet from my resting place. The awesome peaks and mountain valleys of Montana's mountains competed with grand ocean views as we traveled down the west coast. Rugged Oregon headlands filled me with a sense of vastness and grandeur. My definition of "beautiful" expanded in every direction. Here was my new god.

I was introduced to San Francisco and Berkeley with its hippie culture. Ford and I determined to go back to Milwaukee and earn enough money to move out to the west coast as soon as possible. I bought a hippie van. Josie decided to go on the pill, and the day she began, we had sex.

Josie

Only a few weeks later, Josie became pregnant! I learned the news from her father. Icy with rage, he told me that he was trying to get me charged with statutory rape. Josie was to get an abortion. My role was to pay for it. As for me, I did not think of the fetus as a living being. All I knew was that I was only a child myself. What was I to do with a new baby in my life? I paid for the abortion with earnings I made as a longshoreman.

While my attraction towards Josie was waning, I felt responsible for her and for what had happened between us. It did not even enter my mind to grieve for the lost child! Only much later did that happen, when I came to realize that the abortion had been a violent and ugly act. While it was out of sight and so relatively sanitized for me, it had been a terrible trauma for Josie.

I stayed with Josie despite my mixed feelings, and after some sharp prodding from my sister, Mary, I proposed marriage to her. We got married in a classic hippie ceremony, far from the city on a bluff above the shores of Long Lake in central Wisconsin. The vows were a polemic for free love and a denial that it was possible to make a lifetime commitment to anybody.

Those words in our vows came true only a few years later when we divorced. What a foolish thing, that marriage! Neither of us ever truly met the other! The memories now are uniformly sad.

But before the divorce, Ford, Josie and I moved from Milwaukee to Eugene, Oregon, the hippie center of what was beginning to be called Ecotopia, the Pacific Northwest. There we helped form a new tree-planting crew. We called it Pot Luck, first come first served — or did it have to do with smoking marijuana? It depended on who you were in the crew. We joined an umbrella cooperative named after the original tree-planting tool, the hoedad. The Hoedads contract committee funneled Forest Service and Bureau of Land Management tree-planting contracts to about fifteen crews. All of us were hippies.

Josie and I get married

I bought a school bus, and the three of us tore down an old, leaning barn near Eugene for its beautifully silvered siding. With the wood gained from the demolition, we built the inside of the bus into a classic hippie vehicle. It was a work of art topped by a huge roof deck, my home for those hippie years.

As a member of a "Hoedad" crew, we moved all over the American west, planting between 200 and 1000 trees per day. I guess that I planted well over 75,000 trees during those years. In the winter months, we focused on the coast ranges of Oregon, Washington, and northern California. When spring arrived, we moved to the Rocky Mountain forests of Montana, Idaho, Wyoming and Colorado.

Early in the morning before dawn, I would roll out of my sleeping bag and, shivering in my long-johns, start a fire in the little pot-bellied woodstove. There was never a problem about access to firewood, surrounded as we were with the remains of the forest. Next, I fried up a mess of sliced potatoes on the Coleman stove, throwing

My Hoedad years as a tree planter

My Hoedad crew "Pot Luck." That's me at the lower right corner

some eggs on top. Cowboy coffee heated up on the other burner. A raw egg on top settled the grounds, making it ready to blow and sip. At about the same time the potatoes and eggs were ready.

In later years, we cooked cooperatively. Each day the group paid a kitchen person to make breakfast, bag lunches (I fondly remember these thick-slabbed mustard, cheese, and cabbage sandwiches!) and construct a big evening meal. We sat around in the crew teepee or yurt, clean straw spread over the muddy ground beneath our feet and listened to guitar renditions of favorite songs or just talked. I saw it as the good life.

The central Oregon Cascades were the center of our operations. There were several hot springs there, and we used them often. I loved to lay in the piping hot water until my heart started pounding. Then I rolled over the loose stone wall separating the hot spring water from the mountain stream and slid into the icy cold, fast-flowing water. After a few minutes and some strong hyperventilation in the creek, I stretched out on one of the great Douglas fir trunks that surrounded the spring and relaxed in the misty rain.

When we were far from access to hot springs, we made sweat lodges. Early in the morning, a crew member would select some big, solid rocks (not river rocks, for they would explode) and lined the base of a big fire pit with them. A roaring fire was built over them and then allowed to burn down to a massive bed of coals. The whole fire was covered with dirt for three or four hours.

In the eve-
ning, a few of us
cut and bent half
a dozen saplings
and formed a
domed structure.
We stretched
thick blankets and
tarps over it all
and made a little
flap door. When
the rocks were red

Myself and two other crew members
outside our portable yurt

hot, they were dug up and carried with a shovel into the dark little
dome and dropped into a small pit dug in the center of the floor.
Everybody stripped, got inside, sprinkled a bit of water and spread
a few cedar leaves over the rocks and soaked up the intense steam.
The sauna was built right next to a creek, so when we couldn't
take it anymore, we would roll out of the sauna and flop into the
icy cold creek. Yahoo! What a rush and a deep cleansing! These
were happy times.

Then there was the other side of the job. Back at work, encased
in green rubber rain suits over polypropylene long johns, we slid
through the mud and charred remains of hundreds of burned
over logging units. The devastated remains of the forest after
the big Douglas Fir tree trunks had been dragged up out of the
draws supported my opinions about civilization in general. It was
a landscape that suited my blasted, embittered world view.

Contemplating these war zone landscapes, I imagined how
the massive logs had been hauled away to make obese houses for
fat people, stuffed with too much food and too many possessions.
Almost everyone did not know about these places. The real consequences of their lifestyles were carefully hidden away from view.
Only we tree planters, starting a hundred-year healing cycle with

A clearcut "unit" ready to be burned

our little tree seedlings and living in the rain next to these moonscapes, could appreciate the real price paid for those neat stacks of boards for sale in lumber yards all over America. From the air, the whole Pacific Northwest looked like a crazy quilt, but there were carefully preserved "scenic corridors" along all the highways, so tourists did not have their sensibilities offended.

And over the years, healing happened. Bitterness gradually diminished. Slowly, the heavy physical work and the severe wet and cold conditions did their healing work on me. A new aliveness grew in my heart as I watched the morning mists move through cedar trees that edged the devastation and witnessed the sun cut through rain clouds and light up the whole sky, making the ocean in the distance sparkle. I was living simply amidst clearing skies, far from the darkness of the city.

My mind began to clear as well. And as I cleared, the ideals that motivated me quietly changed as well. The time came when it was no longer enough to be "Mr. Natural." Living in the woods and being isolated from society in general meant holding the whole world at arm's length outside of my little group. Every time I went into the city, everybody else seemed to be living in a different universe! I discovered that I was quite a social animal! Putting trees in the ground year after year did not sit well with my intellect and desire to make a difference in the world. I was just too ambitious.

Over the years as a tree planter, I had slowly gained auto and truck repair experience working on crew vehicles. When an opportunity came, I joined a small car repair cooperative called

Car-Tune-Ists. It was an offshoot of Hoedads: most of the early jobs were repairing the cooperative's forest vehicles.

Me and my long-suffering brothers

And so, I moved into an urban hippie house in Eugene. Individuals rented rooms while we all equally shared overhead costs. Almost all of us were tree planters or former tree planters, so there were shared values among us. The big backyard was filled with fruit trees and the front with hippie vans, campers, and school buses. Meanwhile, I rode a bicycle to the shop each day. Overall, the arrangement seemed to work out well.

After a year turning wrenches as a mechanic, I took on the role of office manager, focusing on customer contact and keeping our complex double-entry bookkeeping system up to date. Life was still bleak, and I was poor, but things were bearable.

4

Love's Healing

And there I met my future wife, Joan. She was friends with another man who shared our little house, and when a room became available, she came to "interview." She was attending the University of Oregon towards a degree in environmental education. She moved in, and our relationship quickly deepened.

It seemed to happen naturally, without effort, almost by accident. I had not been in a relationship with a woman since Josie four years before. It wasn't that I hadn't tried, but something always seemed to get in the way. Some of the other female roommates laughed at me, telling me that I appeared to be oblivious to the attentions of the women around me.

But Joan was different. I first met her while standing in the kitchen washing dishes. Looking at her, I recognized a soul mate. It felt appropriate right from the start that we would be lovers. Looking back, I can see that the connection was so rapid that it never allowed the development of our abilities to communicate, much to our detriment years later when we seemed to lack essential tools to understand and talk about the changes that were

Joan, my wife of 25 years

then withering our relationship. Being in a relationship together had been effortless at first, so when it became otherwise, we had no tools to deal with the change.

Those early years of our relationship brought happiness into my life on a whole new level. Joan was easy, peaceful and relaxed about the details of life, a natural phlegmatic. Even when I tested her with criticism, she took it in as a phase I needed to go through rather than taking it personally. After a few months, we moved into a little house closer to the campus, renting out a few rooms to other college students to make the rent.

I decided to quit Hoedads. Forty-five minutes later, I had a job doing landscaping. I also decided to go to the local Community College and study landscape development, a one-year program. There was a simple rhythm and ease to my life as the hard physical work, and the genuine intimacy of loving Joan healed me deep inside.

After Joan graduated, we moved to Oakridge, a small town 45 miles to the southeast of Eugene in the middle of the Cascade Mountains. I worked first at a tree seedling nursery, then as a trail crew boss, all-around carpenter and weekend district guard for the Forest Service, while Joan worked as a silvicultural assistant, quantifying biomass out in the vast Oregon forests.

We lived together for about three years before we married in a simple ceremony at her parent's home in Michigan. We wrote the ceremony ourselves, and it closed as I stamped on a little wine glass inside a velvet envelope and we shouted "Mazeltov!" led by her delighted grandparents.

We bought a little rundown place on five acres near Oakridge. Over the three years we lived there, I completely remodeled the

house, rebuilding large parts of
the foundation and the second
floor. I also renovated an old der-
elict outbuilding, turning it into a
beautiful 1000-square-foot shop.
We built a large fenced garden and
pumped water up from the creek
that flowed through the center of
the property to irrigate it. It was
a beautiful place. The remodeling
kept me busy during the off-season
winter months, and the dignity of

Working for the Forest Service in
the Cascades and in our first home

owning the place grounded me in satisfaction. I cut and split wood
for heat, we baked our bread, and we grew vegetables in the large
garden. It was a settler life, straight out of the TV westerns I used
to love as a child.

Again, our fantasies around the "good life" wore thin after a
few years as we both began to feel too isolated from the world. We
weren't making much money with the Forest Service and felt the
pinch of our meager finances. Near the end of the three years that
we lived there, we were becoming homesick for city life again.

One day I was sitting on the back porch, bone tired from a day
of hauling firewood. I found myself deeply moved by the sunset
beauty of this little piece of the world. The physical peace of a
hard day's work and the beauty of the place struck a deep chord
in my heart. I watched the little creek flowing through our yard
as it passed under our little bridge. The sun shone through the
massive hemlocks stretching up the hill across the creek. There
was a feeling of completion and peace.

But I also recognized that a significant part of myself could
not rest here. Perhaps someday I could return to this place of
simplicity, but in the meantime, I had to learn some basic lessons
out there somewhere in the world, lessons about who I was, what

I was capable of doing, what it all meant. I yearned to use my newfound spiritual and mental health to explore and connect with the world. Perhaps someday I could return to this place, but first, there was work to do.

Not a long time later, we decided together to attend university. Joan wanted to go back for a second degree in occupational therapy. I didn't know where it would go for me, but when I imagined going to university, it no longer seemed like a copout. Now it appeared to have potential as an excellent adventure. Joan thought that the OT Program at the University of Washington was the best choice. I said, "Sure, why not?" I applied and was accepted. We moved to Seattle.

Seattle was such a different world! The city itself was full of intensity, excitement, and beauty, while beautiful landscape views could be found in every direction. To the east, the snow covered North Cascades dominated the horizon. To the west, spread above the waters of Puget Sound rose the mighty Olympic Mountains. To the south lay the immense volcanic cone of slumbering Mount Rainier.

The University was one big flower garden and arboretum. It was built along an axis that put Mount Rainier's snow cone in the center of the view, all framed by classic Neo-Gothic quads. Portage Bay and Lake Union stretched away from the southern edge of the campus. The place was truly splendid.

So was the world of academia. It all seemed to be an immense gift to me! I studied diligently and found a new peace in the disciplined, focused, almost monastic existence of

The University of Washington Campus Quad

a serious student. We lived in a beautiful, colonnaded third story apartment we got for a song, surrounded by lush plane trees. For the first time, I felt part of a human community that was beautiful and rich with meaning.

In College, age thirty-Four

Jogging in the early mornings around Pioneer Park up on Capitol Hill, I drank in the feeling of shared experience with the other joggers and nearby residents. I joined a rowing club and began to row regularly, getting up in the pre-dawn darkness to bike down to the University to join four or eight-person crews for a row at dawn. Pulling back hard and smooth on my oar, I watched the dawn unfurl each morning. The needle-like hull would skim across the glassy surface of Portage Bay while only the deep, even sounds of our breathing and the water sliding off the lifting oars broke the silence.

Joan was supremely at home in the academic environment, and she enjoyed her occupational therapy coursework. We spent many happy hours in conversation about our subjects. We also spent happy hours with her parents, whom I grew to love and cherish as my own. Her father was a physiology professor at the University of Illinois and her mother an ethnomusicologist specializing in the study of Arapaho music. Cultured and articulate, they gracefully welcomed me into their home and lives. They were nonjudgmental and broad-minded, in stark contrast to many Christians I had met since I had left the Lord.

I spent hundreds of hours in the vast Suzzallo Reading Room at the main library. Sitting at one of the long tables with its built-in light bar, I would look up from my work and scan the great, echoing

The Suzallo Reading Room at the UW Library

room, tracing the buttress arches that laced the ceiling or enjoying the huge stained glass windows that lined both sides of the room. There was a pure quality to the light. In fact, the place was a cathedral to me.

Of course, the room was intended to generate such perceptions. Its designers reflected the belief that accumulated human knowledge was the most precious thing imaginable and that enlightened modern beings should worship knowledge in the same way that the superstitious had once worshiped God. To me, it heralded the transfer of allegiance from the old traditional gods of the past, to the one true modern god, Reason.

Having been trained in the way of faith, it was not difficult for me to take up their subliminal suggestions. I became a believer. Old connections with something so much greater than I — God — became intertwined with a new desire to worship the vast knowledge storehouse that humans had built up over the centuries.

The ideal world of Reason was a heady dream indeed. Here was a tool so powerful that we could create a whole new world! And not just more of everything, but a quantum leap from the old Dark Ages when we continually submitted to some unknowable, harsh judging father god. Instead, we could work together using our minds to build a civilization that was fair and honest and powerful beyond our greatest expectations.

I began my studies with the clearly-stated desire to explore knowledge for knowledge's sake. I sincerely appreciated the beauty and symmetry of the intellect. An idealist, I roamed the class catalogs each quarter looking for what I thought could expand my mind. I studied world history, macroeconomic history, formal logic, pre-Socratic philosophy, linguistics, psychology, sociology, architecture, astronomy and many other subjects.

I especially was fascinated with religious history, both East and West. Never had I closely looked at religion in a scientific, historical way with sensitivity for its social context. I surmised that much of the religious urge could be explained by the great human need to feel in control, to define and box the otherwise indefinable. I studied the early years of our country and learned that a central motivation for the creation of the earliest English settlements was the desire to practice religious freedom.

The dominant paradigm of those early American years was the desire to build a special "city on a hill," as the Puritans put it, a physical place where heaven could come to earth, and real righteousness could be practiced. Even in those early days of America, most believers knew that such a city ultimately was to be built on the pragmatic and mundane building blocks of hard work and independent trade. Regarding brick and stone, it was a world of reason upon which that city was to be built.

As I progressed through the quarters, I began to realize that I was excellent at this! A new edge entered my life as I began to compete with myself to get top grades. Eventually, I turned it into a marathon, graduating summa cum laude and with departmental honors. I was in the top half of the top 1% in a pool of 5,000 graduates!

Arriving in the New World, ready to build that city

Mom at my graduation in 1987
just a year before she passed away

Success infused me with a new self-confidence, but I didn't have a clue what I would do to make a living with my new degree. Neither Joan nor I could imagine returning to our old way of life. We were both interested in greater income and living a little more comfortably.

I struggled to decide what to do next. I took a course in career opportunities, completing the Myers-Briggs Personality Inventory and several other personality evaluation tests. The climax of the course was the production of a printout listing about a dozen jobs that suited my talents well. I decided one of these careers was to be my future.

Psychologist, high school teacher, professor, attorney, physical therapist, occupational therapist: all these occupations were on the list. The word "attorney" jumped out at me. Here there were a lot of possibilities for different specialties. High status and good money were associated with it. Joan liked the idea, as did her parents. And so, the decision was made. It was that simple. I began seeking out information about law schools.

5

Making a
Better World

I knew it was a long shot to apply at Berkeley, but I did anyway, despite dismissing the possibility of getting in as vanishingly small. Berkeley Admissions only allowed a quarter of the class to be from out of state, and there were some thirty applicants for every slot. Meanwhile, I got into several other good schools, including Columbia, NYU, and UW, but the whole thing jelled the day I got an acceptance letter from Berkeley. While rated as being in the top 2% of all law schools in stature, its cost of attendance was in the bottom 2%. As far as I was concerned, it was a no-brainer.

We boxed our few possessions and drove a U-Haul van from our beautiful Seattle to Berkeley. What a shock it was after our idyllic time in Seattle! "Berzerkely" was in your face: politicized, radicalized, dirty, anti-business, its urban development atrophied by socialist city planning. But it was filled with brilliant, idiosyncratic, interesting people. Nobel laureates had a row of parking spaces reserved for them right near the Law School.

UC Berkeley is one of the very best public universities in the country. Its programs rank in the top tier across the board, including both the hard sciences and the social sciences. It thrived on political and social dissent and was nationally known for its tolerance for radicalism. The place birthed the Free Speech Movement of the early 60s when naked students protested everything including civilization itself. Meanwhile, across the Bay Bridge, the Beat Generation gave way to San Francisco's Summer of Love in 1967. Does any of this sound familiar? I should have been totally at home.

But I wasn't. I had changed. I found a streak of middle-class "bourgeois" sensibility woven through my character. "Where did this come from?" I asked. I was from a more "standard" stamp than I had realized. I recoiled from the extremist, relentless modernity of the Bay Area. People here were willing to throw out things that I found sacred.

To say that it was very different from the relatively buttoned-down scene in Seattle was an understatement. A few days after our arrival, we took our first trip across the Bay to San Francisco, using the beautiful Bay Area Rapid Transit System or BART. We climbed the stairs out of the subway terminal and into downtown San Francisco, finding ourselves in the center of the annual Gay Pride parade. Soon both of us sported saucer eyes. We felt like we had landed on a different planet! Crowds of men marched by in leather chaps — and nothing else! Men and women pulled their mates along by dog leashes attached to their loved one's neck. Semi-nude women dressed as nuns whipped the crowd with feathery boa whips. The afternoon parade was totally in our faces, with overt manifestations of all sorts of sexualities! The spectacle overwhelmed us.

We had difficulty finding a good place to live. Finally, at the last minute, we became roommates in a lovely house just a few blocks from the law school. But it was a disaster. The other two roomies were both women going through personal crises. One had a volatile personality and was in the middle of a messy breakup with her husband. Her five-year-old child was relentlessly acting out, intensely distraught with the loss of his father. The other, an emergency room nurse, had a two-year-old girl who was going through the terrible twos. Joan and I were overwhelmed by the intensity of emotion going on in the house. We moved out after the first semester. It was a very trying time for both of us.

Meanwhile, at school, I had gone from an academic environment I loved to one that was confusing, intimidating and ultimately repellent. In early writing projects, my complex, colorful sentences were relentlessly lampooned. These dinosaurs were to be dumped, replaced with short declarative sentences that built the client's arguments like bricks in a stone wall. I eventually got the hang of it: In my second year, I placed first in my advanced legal research class with a 120-page literature survey of the growing right of psychiatric patients to refuse medication. But while I was good at

doing these things, I felt like classes taught me to dissect the subtleties of life into commodities to sell them to the highest bidder.

I had thought I was a pretty logical guy. But that was before I studied torts, the area of the law

compensating those whose legally protected interests were harmed. My torts professor taught this field of law in a "revolutionary" new way. Unfortunately, his revolution made absolutely no sense to me! I struggled painfully through the course, passing the final exam primarily because the prof knew I had put enormous effort into my ultimately futile attempts to understand his revolution. Meanwhile, I did well in the nuts and bolts courses.

Many of my classmates were brilliant young lions, eager for big paychecks. Many seemed to glory in their newfound freedom to pick a position — any position — and then find a legal foundation for it. I met more than a few students with gargantuan egos during those years. But there was a small group, many of them older, that I began to call friends.

Summer work was both lucrative and uninspiring. My first summer, I worked in one of San Francisco's oldest firms, a traditional bastion specializing in banking law. My performance was adequate, but I didn't want to pursue that further. My second summer I worked for a hip boutique firm evenly divided between business law, focusing on the art of the deal, and litigation, the art of suit and counter-suit. I signed up for litigation work at the firm. But when I was offered a position at the end of the summer, I wasn't excited by the prospect of further employment.

I found my meaning in the clinical externships, experiences that offered real life advocacy out in the community. I found myself especially excited by a clinical with the nearby Martineztown Public Defenders office. I appreciated the loner, cowboy-like character of the defense attorneys. Defense attorneys often stood alone, their professional efforts spelling the difference between freedom and incarceration for their clients. Much of the legal side of the work involved defending personal protections written into the US Constitution. Here was a niche where I could thrive!

While I completed my Juris Doctor at UC Berkeley, Joan got a master's degree in occupational therapy at the University of

San Francisco, a Jesuit
school across the bay.
Following our gradu-
ations, we sat down to
figure out what to do
next. First, we chose
our favorite region in
the country in which
to live. After chewing
over all the possibili-

ties, we came to Albuquerque, New Mexico. It offered beautiful
scenery and a pleasant, mild climate, along with some of the most
diverse cultures in America. There was also a well-respected university there where Joan hoped eventually to teach.

I quickly passed the New Mexico bar, and we drove a U-Haul
across the desert to our new home. Shortly after our arrival, I found
a position representing juveniles with the Albuquerque office of
the New Mexico State Public Defender.

I worked in the trenches of Juvenile Court there for almost ten
years, completing about 4,000 cases. The work was wonderfully
fulfilling. For many years, I could not imagine doing anything else.

Early each morning, I would check in at the Juvenile Detention
Center to talk to new clients, kids that had been arrested the day
before and held in detention pending a hearing. The most severe
cases started with the urgent task of trying to get the client released
pending resolution of the charges. What an amazing group of
handcuffed young people walked into that place!

At one end of the spectrum were young "throwaway" kids
who had been neglected and abused by drug-addicted or alcoholic
parents. A throwaway kid might be a danger to himself, perhaps
for something like "huffing," breathing in aerosol paint fumes
sprayed into a paper bag. There was little that the system could
offer them. They were often quickly released to their so-called

parents. A lot of these kids were on their way to frying their brains and looked forward to life at the bottom of the societal heap — or even worse, as convicts.

At the other end of the spectrum were cool-eyed senior gang members who had done it all and gotten away with most of it. Gangs were ubiquitous, multi-generational and efficient at what they did. Gang bangers organized residential burglaries and drug sales to generate income. There were lots of inter-gang fights arising out of turf wars. Making quick money made sense to kids who didn't see many other options. Many of them had left school or were just scraping by. "Bangers" sometimes came from families where their parents and even grandparents had been gang members. In those neighborhoods, the gang was just a basic way of life. They had taken on a worldview that seemingly gave them hope, but in the end, many ended disabled in some way, dead or incarcerated. The justice system spent plenty of money on this increasingly dangerous group, but positive outcomes, both in reduced recidivism and improved lives, was spotty at best.

Most of the kids detained pending trial were poor blacks or Hispanics. Blacks comprised a tiny minority in Albuquerque but were over-represented in the Juvenile Justice System. Studies showed that blacks were far more likely to be presented with worst-case scenarios at every step of the system. From suspicion-based surveillance, pushy, even violent interrogation methods and quick arrests to routine initial detentions and long incarcerations before trial all led the way to more serious outcomes at trials and sentencing hearings. Racism was woven deeply into the system. These kids endured grueling, often crushing challenges.

The first cases on the court's calendar always addressed whether those detained within the last day (or over the weekend) were released pending trial. This was often a time of fast dealing with the prosecuting Juvenile Court Attorneys. If a child was held, they could remain detained up to a month or longer. One client detained on a gang-related murder charge was held over a year before his case resolved.

Regular court sessions followed, usually taking the rest of the morning. Cases involving first-time offenders ended with formal warnings or short periods of probation followed by a dismissal of the charges. Other cases, especially involving kids with multiple referrals to the system, involved more complex, lengthy probation agreements. These could include requirements for various forms of community service, counseling for youth or family issues, voluntary drug or alcohol treatment, mandatory completion of anti-gang programs or even special concentrated electronic surveillance during probation.

I loved the pure speed of the job. Once I knew the ropes, I moved at top speed, pumping through the day on adrenaline, persuading the court to release clients at detention hearings, putting to rest several cases during morning court sessions and spending the afternoon writing motions, studying new cases, or negotiating with prosecutors. I tried hard to make good deals for my clients. I wanted to do the best job possible.

Serious cases required the filing of motions, witness interviews and many hearings leading up to jury trials. I defended clients before the court on charges involving violence, including murder, rape and aggravated battery. The most serious plea agreement I facilitated was a guilty plea to first-degree murder with a sentence of 30 years to have about 15 years of other charges dismissed. This plea was later vacated; then, after hiring one of the most prominent defense attorneys in the state, the young man was found guilty by a jury and sentenced to the same thirty plus fourteen years more.

My team of Juvenile Public Defenders

Our relationship with the private bar was complicated. We didn't make much money, and they most certainly did, but we often saw our work as being of better quality than theirs. After working a complicated murder case for about a year, we negotiated a plea to 2nd-degree murder with a guarantee of 7 years. With good time and time served, the client was looking at less than two years in prison. But the child's mother stopped the proceedings minutes before the plea was taken. She had been talking to "Neon Leon," a local attorney with a gilded reputation. We walked away from the case while the family put a $30,000 second mortgage on their home to pay for the trial to come. In the end, he was found guilty and sentenced to 14 years!

One of my greatest triumphs was co-defending a murder case. The young lady charged with the offense received a complete acquittal at the end of a long jury trial. I prided myself on doing the utmost for my clients every day, sometimes spending lots of time on one at the expense of others. It was plain that some kids coming in with many prior referrals to the system had never received the kind of close attention to their circumstances that were necessary to craft a "treatment plan" that had a real chance to change their attitudes and behavior. These cases demanded real digging and solid argument during sentencing.

Every once-in-awhile an intervention in a child's life bore fruit; news of a graduation or testimony about a changed life circulated through the courthouse, raising our spirits and providing new energy for what was often thankless work. The caseload was high, but with the proper effort I kept up with the work without exhausting myself.

I loved this work because of its immersion in roiling, suffering humanity, as well as its challenging and exacting routines. Over time, intimate glimpses into the family lives of thousands of young people brought a new perspective on my history. What I had lived through was a small matter compared to some of the hells these kids experienced! I realized deep in my heart that my life could have been much worse, and for the first time I was thankful for what had been my lot in life.

My heart stretched as it connected with these young men and women. Empathy for their suffering and a larger compassion for the world in general grew in my heart. As I stood next to my clients in court, I too experienced the emotional impact of their losses of innocence — and sometimes of hope — as they headed toward more probation, reformatories and for some, an adult prison.

Sometimes I seemed more affected by sentencing outcomes than my clients. The chief prosecutor, with whom I worked daily, remarked several times that I acted as if I was the one charged with the crimes, not my clients! I keenly felt their trauma with them as they were sentenced, as they walked out the back door of the courtroom with the sheriff deputy's hand on their shoulder, as they were manacled in the back hall, as they were led to anonymous vans and driven away to remote institutions. I could go home after the hearings, but sometimes I felt like the walking wounded.

There were many heartbreaking stories. Slowly it became harder to stand next to some young man with an increasingly fatalistic attitude who was going down on yet another delinquent charge or listen to another story describing horrifying home circumstances. Victims' sad and sometimes sickening stories brought a growing belief in the futility of their suffering. It seemed that the only options for child victims of poverty, drugs and gang violence were meaningless, dead-end jobs or incarceration.

Of course, there were exceptions — stories of somebody who fought against the stream of his circumstances and won — but these were rare. It broke my heart to see so many examples of the relentless downward pull of that which was clearly beyond the control of these young men and women, the circumstances of their birth.

Meanwhile, I spent my days arguing for fairness and equal access to justice. I made many foolish decisions when I was their age, just as they had, but I had been protected from the punitive consequences they were experiencing by positive circumstances beyond my control, especially my race. How could this world even imagine itself to be fair or just?

In the mid-nineties, the prosecutor's office was injected with large amounts of new funding and hired several new prosecutors. The Public Defender's office did not receive similar funding increases. The caseload balance moved dramatically in favor of the prosecution. My workload shot up from three or four hundred to almost eight hundred cases a year. The job became even more stressful, as time constraints precluded me from doing the extra work that had been a constant part of caseload management beforehand and brought a big part of my personal satisfaction. I began to show increasing symptoms of stress.

Kindness

Before you know what kindness is,
You must lose things,
Feel the future dissolve in a moment
Like salt in a weakened broth.
What you held in your hand,
What you counted and carefully saved,
All this must go so you know
How desolate the landscape can be
Between the regions of kindness.
How you ride and ride
Thinking the bus will never stop,
The passengers eating maize and chicken
Will stare out of the window forever.

Before you learn the tender gravity of kindness,
You must travel where the Indian in the white poncho
Lies dead by the side of the road.
You must see how this could be you,
How he too was someone
Who journeyed through the night with plans
And a simple breath that kept him alive.

Before you know kindness as the deepest thing inside,
You must know sorrow is the other deepest thing;
You must wake up with sorrow,
You must speak to it till your voice
Catches the thread of the sorrows
And you see the size of the cloth.

Then it is only kindness that makes sense anymore,
Only kindness that ties your shoes
And sends you out into the day
To mail letters and purchase bread;
Only kindness that raises its head
From the crowd of the world to say,
"It is I that you have been looking for,"
And then goes with you everywhere
Like a shadow or a friend.

by Naomi Shihab-Nye

While I was immersed in the high tension, high-speed circus of
Juvenile Court, Joan grew into her new role as a lecturer in the
occupational therapy program at the University of New Mexico.

The University environment was fast paced but measured, without regular emotional upheaval.

Our marriage had always revolved around our shared interests. The willingness and capability to share our lives depended on everyday experiences. As the years went by, our common ground seemed to recede.

We cared about each other and certainly enjoyed each other's company when we met at home after a day's work. But I was filled with stories of the sad lives of my clients and the sometimes desperate tactics I used in Children's Court. Joan, on the other hand, was writing grants, tutoring students or brainstorming new teaching techniques — a very different world.

Strains began to appear. The first fifteen years of marriage had been almost effortless, for we got along well and hardly ever argued. Now difficult things had to be said and profound new connections needed to be forged, yet neither of us was willing, or seemingly able, to engage the other. By the time the need became apparent, a conspiracy of silence had grown between us.

I isolated myself during off-times, focusing on remodeling our home. Joan spent weekends away shopping or spent hours in the kitchen cooking. The quality of our communication slowly, inexorably decreased.

At the same time, our mutual interest in Buddhism and the spiritual life in general increased, perhaps as compensation for the creeping coldness of our vitiated relationship. Buddhism offered a coolness and peace, a release from all this inherently messy emotion. Its rewards came from its main behavioral activity: meditation practice. Meditation delivered a sense of relaxation and a felt reduction in daily stress levels. The Buddha just said: "Come and see."

6

Leaving the World

I began participating in silent 10-day meditation retreats in the early '80s, following Joan's positive report about her experiences. They offered a sequestered environment, often in beautiful natural settings, which focused on complete concentration — sitting and walking meditation. Retreat routines were very similar. One rose at 4 or 5 in the morning and spent the day alternating sessions of 45 minutes sitting and walking meditation practice. There were breaks for vegetarian meals and a period in the early afternoon for a bit of a nap. There was an hour or so of discussion of basic Buddhist theory, called Dhamma talks, each evening.

Retreats were beautiful escapes from the tense, frenetic, multitasking world of Juvenile Court. They were much-appreciated vacations. But they were also much more than that: I often experienced great releases during the retreat, as was the case for many other beginning practitioners. These cycles of suffering and release created opportunities for deep reflection and change. Through work and meditation, my inner world slowly deepened.

At home, Joan and I cultivated the habit of sitting quietly for about an hour each day. I made a little wooden bench so that I could sit kneeling on the front of my forelegs as they were tucked beneath the angled sitting shelf. I also sat on a round cushion called a zafu.

Then we followed the simple instructions: sit quietly and comfortably, back erect but not tense. Strive to remove the internal comment and simply watch the inhalation and the exhalation of the breath at the tip of the nose. Most of my meditation sessions probably looked good externally, but internally I would frantically try to hang on for the wild ride as my mind leaped from memory to memory, frantically searching for the slightest possibility of present-time sensory input. At retreats, the mind ran amok; racing through all kinds of fantasies, and paranoias. Most meditation sessions during those early years were chock full of this kind of "thinking." Sometimes a meditation would devolve into quiet disassociation, and I would wake up 45 minutes later wondering where the time had gone. For some time, I thought of this kind of meditation space as a "good sit" because the session went by so fast and with little physical pain from kneeling.

When I found myself completely overloaded during the first year of Law School in 1990, I dropped my daily meditation practice, and it wasn't until the mid-nineties that I returned. But even during this hiatus, Joan and I loved to read, and our mutual subject of choice was often contemporary western Buddhism.

This time, we began to seek out meditation groups with whom we could develop fellowship and discuss Buddhist teachings. We also came into regular contact with several people who were quite adept at delivering "Dhamma talks." Our knowledge and interest in Buddhism deepened. We eventually became the focal point of one such group, and I played a role in that group's effort to gain non-profit corporate status.

As the decade ended, our lives were grounded in the Buddhist worldview. Our "double-income-no-kids" status had made us physically comfortable as our assets continued to increase. But our personal financial successes paled in importance as we took on Buddhist values. Possessions were encumbrances that weighed us down, tying us again and again to rebirth. What was the point of it all? The life of a full-time Buddhist practitioner began to appear more and more attractive.

The Buddhist worldview, at least superficially, was easy to understand. The idea of reincarnation was simple: a "revolving door" world of birth, death, and rebirth made logical sense to me as I observed the overwhelming power that each person's unique circumstances and personality had on the shape of their lives. Virtuous or non-virtuous behavior had consequences in this present-time life. If one lived a moral life, one traveled in future rebirths towards increasingly refined heaven worlds. Similarly, if one acted without virtue, then rebirth into various hells was the natural result.

But as I understood the concept in a deeper way, I realized that there was an arbitrary undercurrent to it. Over endless cycles of birth, death, and rebirth, the power of one's good or bad acts ebbed and flowed, moving one up or down, from heaven to hell and back again, like waves washing up on a timeless shore. One simile in Buddhist scripture describes rebirth outcomes as almost random, as a thrown stick might land on either end or even the middle. Only very occasionally does one pass through this uniquely propitious human world where virtue and its lack, as well as pain and pleasure, are balanced sufficiently to allow meditation practice — and allow a radical new way out.

By ceasing to attach to anything at all through extended meditation practice, the mind could "release" from the endless cycle and entered a state of original purity, free from all encumbrances: liberation. I found this most intriguing.

As I more deeply understood- and believed — the Buddhist worldview, I became increasingly dissatisfied with my life "in the world." As a Public Defender, it often seemed that for every step forward, I was taking two steps back. The same kids appeared and re-appeared before the Court, and it appeared that there was nothing the system could offer that was robust enough to decisively and successfully intervene in their lives. Conditions of birth appeared to be the determinative factor in whether a kid made it or not. I was just spinning my wheels. I felt increasingly rudderless, drifting, without purpose or meaning.

The tension in my heart from the early days was buffered by education, income, and meaningful work, but I was still loaded down by an internal spiritual pressure I could not name but felt every day. I started getting therapeutic massages every week, and in these two-hour sessions, I would weep uncontrollably as my muscles were moved. I would jokingly say, "Here comes The Screamer" as I would come in to see Angela for another session. The uncapped pain did not have a name except "pain" or "grief." This went on for over a year. Finally, it somehow became OK to be massaged.

I received shocking news about Ted. I had no contact whatsoever with Ted since the day my mother, my brother and I left him involuntarily committed to the psych ward in Birmingham some 30 years before.

My brother, John, learned of a murder case involving a Leitner that had been big news in central Alabama. Unwilling to do anything himself, he asked me to follow through and see what I could find out. I hired a local Birmingham researcher, who after six months or so sent me a packet of newspaper clippings with datelines stretching over several years. They told the whole story.

Ted had married an elderly blind widow and had used her money to travel around the world indulging his pedophile proclivities with young homeless boys. Eventually, this behavior drew him into a dark love triangle between a street kid he had picked up in Atlanta and a Catholic priest in Tuscaloosa. Stretched to the point of murderous rage by his jealousy, he bludgeoned the priest to death with a galvanized pipe and burned the body in front of the boy. He then threatened the boy who had "helped" him carry out the murder, forcing him into a terrified silence.

Ted quickly returned to the priest's home parish and led the congregants in their search for the missing priest. After police had found the body, there was precious little evidence pointing to anyone as a suspect. But soon Ted got into the habit of asking pointed questions of the detective assigned to the case. After quite a bit of time, the detective began to treat Ted as a suspect. Not long after, the boy was found and through his confession, the case broke open.

Ted was convicted of first-degree murder, but the case was reversed on appeal and remanded for a new trial. The Alabama Supreme Court held that the defense motion asking the trial court to allow the priest's personal diary into evidence had been illegally denied. The Supreme Court published relevant sections of the journal into the record of their decision, one that routinely mailed to all attorneys in the state. The priest's diary reflected the mind of a very, very sick man, a man tormented by guilt and shame.

Ted lost his second trial as well, despite a new defense attorney and a new theory of defense. The sentence this time: life in prison. A few years later, shortly after he heard word that as an imprisoned felon he could not inherit his elderly wife's estate, Ted hung himself with a sheet from the bars of his cell. It was the sad ending of someone the prosecuting attorney had called "the closest thing he had ever seen to the devil incarnate."

Thirty-five years before, I had been adopted by this man and had called him "father" for five years. Despite the abusive nature of our relationship during those years, I had come to love him. As distorted as the relationship was, he had been the only real father I had known during most of the years of my childhood. And I was sure that he had left a trail of victims behind him wherever he had gone. How many times had he attempted suicide before succeeding? He was a victim of his suffering. In the end, he had lost the fight with his demons. In fact, he had become one of them.

Then, brother John's wife Kathy learned that her body was filled with inoperable liver cancer. Fighting every step of the way with chemo and radiation therapies, she stretched out the original eight-week prognosis to a year. But it was an agonizing year for the whole family, including me. Through her slow decline to death, John struggled with grief, loneliness, depression and loss of focus. Kathy had been a very dear friend to me as well. I sorely missed her direct and open-hearted vitality and servant's heart. Her death seemed random, senseless, without meaning. Life was not fair, and it could all change in a flash.

And then another death came, this time a close colleague. A Juvenile Division social worker just didn't wake up on the morning of her 50th birthday, dying of a sudden heart attack. She had been in reasonably good health, so her death was completely unexpected.

All this loss struck my heart with great force. Then my Dad died. Mother quietly passed away in the late eighties after a decade-long bout with lymphoma and leukemia. Dad's second wife, my stepmother Dinah, had been a calming, quieting influence on Dad, but in the early nineties she had a stroke and died shortly after that. After her death, he began to change. He gave away almost everything he had—including his home—to a homeless Hispanic family migrating to the western states looking for work, and then one day he disappeared with them. My family lost track of Dad's whereabouts.

A few months later we were contacted by the American Consulate in Guadalajara. They had news about Dad. He had been found dead on the floor of a small, empty apartment. A large purple patch directly over his heart gave direct evidence as to the cause of death. At age 83, Dad's heart had burst.

Hardly a hint
Of their early death.
Cicadas singing
In the trees.

Basho

I was the only member of my family willing and able to go to Mexico and identify his body. Joan and I found his body in a small rural morgue housed in an old gasoline station. The dilapidated building was just across the street from the US — Mexico border, marked by an enormous, twenty-foot-high rusting plate-steel wall that stretched into the distance across the little hills in both directions.

A worker opened an antique glass fronted commercial freezer and removed the cracking clear plastic sheeting from Dad's body. The body was stiff, propped upright in the corner. Yup, it was him, his jaw grotesquely gaping open, his face covered with drops of water. The memory still shocks me. My dad was gone too.

I knew he had not wanted to be embalmed but rather be placed in a simple pine box and buried in a cemetery next to Dinah near his home. Mexican officials told me that I could not take his body out of

Mexico unless it was embalmed, so I was forced to cremate the body. A few days later I walked with the little box — still warm — through the Customs checkpoint and back across the border.

We returned home with his ashes, unsure as to what to do next. For three years, I kept that little white cardboard box of ashes in my living room. Sometimes I opened the box and sifted the finely ground calcium through my fingers. I felt profound emotion at his loss. I knew that there was something important I must do or realize, but I did not have a clue what that might be. So, I kept those ashes, pondering, seeing the white dust of his body on my fingers as I sat by my lamp in the night.

We organized and participated in a New Age/Jewish funeral for him. Then I held a Buddhist funeral. In the center of our meditation room, I placed his ashes inside my meditation bell on top of an elk skull with a candle plunged into the ashes. We chanted and each of us, while holding the ash filled bell, exchanged stories about our grief over departed loved ones. We also recognized and honored our teachers and all the ancient ones who had passed on the Dhamma over the centuries. Finally, we meditated and listened to a talk about impermanence from our beloved Dhamma teacher Eric. A year later, I threw some of Dad's ashes into the Pacific Ocean off the Oregon Coast where he and I had once shared food and the view.

Finally, I came to a place where I could honor him. Finally, I could respect him for the flawed, imperfect, sincere and earnest man he had been. I came to closure. It appeared to me that I looked around my world with a new capacity for vision, for long-distance seeing. I was beginning to heal from the tragedies I experienced as a child, but I kept my belief in God squashed into a place I refused to explore.

Last Days

Walking, I look at this lifted, sweat-bathed hand:
Gray, clabbered skin, liver spots, prominent vein traceries.
Attention bounces between surface and bones beneath;
There's the forefinger stump from the saw accident
And many little white-line scars from years of hard use.
The whole thing perceptibly shakes to a monotonous backbeat.

Dad's hands looked like these.
He had the shakes too; Parkinson's it was.
He could barely sign "Dad" to end his painful typed letters.
Died of a bursting heart awhile back, alone in a Mexican hut.
Nobody knows what happened beyond just that.

And then I abandoned what I thought of as "my life:"
Middle-class, married, professional, money in the bank…
"Already Dead," I thought. And I entered this "Holy Life,"
Or more directly, I abandon everything
Until only the real, the Dhamma remains.

Dad was sure that he had "gotten it."
Preaching yet another canned Luther sermon.
But most folks who knew him were pretty sure he hadn't.
And I still can't get enough of mourning that.

This heart too is clustered with ignorance!
Spiritual urgency burns hard and bright
Inside and around these old bones.
What should I do next to bring Liberation to this aging
Barely sealed sack of skin?

There is nothing like the death of people close to the heart to bring home life's immediacy and the miracle of its everydayness. Life happens breath-by-breath! Death is always only a breath away! There was no time to waste in following my heart!

I became gripped with what in Buddhism is called *samvega* and what Christians can understand through a reading of Ecclesiastes. It's a spiritual urgency brought on by an oppressive, shocking sense of the futility of normal household life, a sense of shame in the face of the daily denial of our spiritual possibilities, combined with faith and hope in the possibility of a higher way to live.

All streams run to the sea, but the sea is not full;
to the place where the streams flow, there they flow again.
All things are full of weariness; a man cannot utter it;
the eye is not satisfied with seeing, nor the ear filled with hearing.
So, what has been is what will be,
and what has been done is what will be done,
and there is nothing new under the sun.

Ecclesiastes 1: 7-9 ESV

I began to dream of myself as a full-time Buddhist practitioner, taking positive steps towards the only goal worth more than nothing. I wanted to stop wasting this precious and finite life and to press towards the deepest, most subtle understanding of Truth I could reach.

The Buddhist worldview had become the way by which I processed reality. It appeared to be scientific, empirically based and logical. Both Joan and I became engrossed with the idea of completely devoting our lives to following the Buddhist path to awakening. Old idealisms were re-awakened, and we began to form concrete plans to follow our dream.

We were both ready to move. We sold the house and our few major possessions, giving away everything else except for a few boxes. We quit our jobs, bought a camper pickup and so set out on our Great Quest. We decided that we were not going to plan much, but act spontaneously, following our ideals down the winding path to liberation.

Until one is committed, there is hesitancy, the chance to draw back, always ineffectiveness. Concerning all acts of initiative (and creation) there is one elementary truth, the ignorance of which kills countless ideas and splendid plans: that the moment one commits oneself, then Providence moves, too. All sorts of things occur to help one that would never otherwise have occurred. A whole stream of events issue from the decision, raising in one's favor all manner of unforeseen incidents and meetings and material assistance, which no man could have dreamed would have come his way.

Until One is Committed by Goethe

As our first post-employment step towards our goal, we both signed up for a three-month silent meditation retreat at a center in the rolling hardwood forests of central Massachusetts.

Insight Meditation Society, Barre, MA

Each day started around 4:30 a.m. with walking meditation, an ultra-slow-motion lifting, moving and placing walking dance. One could easily take several minutes to walk ten feet. This was followed by one hour of sitting meditation. Buttressed by a pad and sitting cushion and wrapped inside a blanket, I continually refocused my attention at the tip of the nose, experiencing the sensation of the incoming and outgoing breath as it touched the skin at the nostrils. After a break for breakfast and a short work period, I was back at it, doing alternating sitting and walking meditation, interrupted only by meals, a short afternoon nap and an evening talk on various Buddhist subjects. The last meditation ended around 10 pm.

Following this unrelenting schedule, I descended into a very intense place. My roommate did not arrive until the end of the

The main hall, Insight Meditation Society

first week, coming in late at night. I awoke in a sweaty panic and stole out of the room. I went to the all-night counselor's room and curled up on her floor in the fetal position, sobbing. I spent most the next six weeks meditating under blankets in a tiny basement room popularly called "the cave" located beneath the main hall. I was barely able to endure being around the other silent meditators. In this environment of extreme sense deprivation, of solitary confinement, I became exquisitely sensitive to the slightest mental impression. Memories became the center of my existence.

I spent two weeks reliving every moment of a teenage love affair that had occurred thirty years before. I relived every moment as if in Technicolor detail. Most vivid of all were the emotions associated with the events. I sobbed uncontrollably at the memories. For two weeks, my life oscillated between the elation of love and the profound, wrenching grief of its loss.

Then, ever so slowly, the memory faded into black and white. It never returned with anything like its former vivid detail. Most importantly, they lost their emotional color. In later years, I still remembered what had happened, but the emotional impact and eventually even the details of those events slowly faded away. I saw that I had processed the memory with its violent, unfelt emotional content sufficiently for it to be integrated back into everything else that was "me." Once integrated, the memory lost its independent vitality, and from there it slipped silently into nothingness, ultimately the essential nature of all things in this world.

If I Can Let Go

If I can let go as the trees,
Let go their leaves so casually one by one,
If I can come to know what they do know:
That Fall is the release, the consummation,
Then fear of time and the uncertain fruit
Would not distemper the great lucid skies.
If I can take the dark with open eyes
And call it seasonal, not harsh or strange,
And tree-like, stand unmoved before the change,
Lose what I lose, to keep what I can keep.
Love will endure if I can let go.

by Mary Sarton

This same process of release occurred again and again. Most of that first retreat was spent pulled into memory after memory. I did precious little noticing of my breath and quite a bit of remembering every detail of the seemingly endless stories packed into my brain. Still, there was a wonderful sense of meaning, of doing something important, that deepened and softened the mind. I believed that the process ultimately brought wisdom instead of despair and confusion. And ever so slowly, the mind clear

The Prayer Tree

When the heart is cut, or cracked or broken,
Do not clutch it.
Let the wound lie open.
Let the wind from the good old sea
Blow in to bathe the wound with salt and let it sting
Let it go.
Let it out.
Let it all unravel.
Let it be free and it can be a path
On which to travel.

by Michael Lurig

Finally, after eighty-six seemingly identical days, the retreat came to an end. I then discovered that for a very modest price the center offered the opportunity to remain living at the Center and practicing full-time. I would be able to participate in a whole year's schedule while continuing the use of the facility between retreats, practicing alone. What a great idea!

When we broke the silence at the end of the retreat, I excitedly told Joan of this excellent opportunity. "And so you will leave me in the lurch!" she cried. Quickly recovering, she denied the truth of what she had said, apologizing for her emotionalism and within a few days decided to join me as a "long-term yogi."

I spent a full fifteen months at the retreat center, silently watching as retreats of varying lengths led by a wide variety of retreat instructors came and went. I also had regular contact with a staff member, who invited me to a nearby Catholic monastery which practiced the Christian equivalent of Buddhist meditation. They called it contemplative prayer. Through this contact, new vigor entered my understanding of Christianity. For the first time in years, I thought about Jesus, his heroic death and the story of his resurrection. Western Buddhist practice taught that there was truth in all spiritual walks, and the Christian message seemed to take on greater depth and profundity through my meditation experiences.

I spent time reading about some of the great Christian mystics like <u>The Cloud of Unknowing</u> by an anonymous 14th-century monk; Meister Eckert; St. John of the Cross; Sister Therese of Avila and others. I also read several writings about contemplative prayer by Father Thomas Keating. I felt that I was not yet able to look into Jesus' eyes, but that the time could come when I would. Buddhism and Christianity took on a new synchronicity.

I enjoyed the simple daily routine of life at the meditation center, spending hundreds of hours meditating. Eventually, I volunteered to tape all the talking sessions for each retreat and so got a ringside seat at the feet of the most popular western Vipassana (or "Insight Meditation") teachers. I was pleased with the arrangement. As each month of full-time meditation practice passed by, I just felt like I wanted more.

Deep as the snow is,
Let me go as far as I can
Till I stumble and fall,
Viewing the white landscape.

Basho

For Joan, it was quite a different story. While she stayed at IMS for six months after the end of the long fall retreat, she was not happy with practice as a full-time lifestyle. While there appeared to be many options for men to continue full-time practice, especially in Asia, there were precious few such opportunities for women.

She got itchy feet. First, she went to a small personal retreat center in the south of England called "The Barn" for several months. Returning from that, she stayed two more months at our Massachusetts retreat center before finally deciding to go back to Albuquerque. We corresponded regularly, but our hopes for the future continued to diverge away from common ground. Soon Joan returned to teaching at the University.

View with a Grain of Sand

We call it a grain of sand,
But it calls itself neither grain nor sand.
It does just fine without a name,
Whether general, particular,
Permanent, passing, incorrect or apt.
Our glance, our touch, mean nothing to it.
It doesn't feel itself seen or touched,
And that it fell on the windowsill
Is only our experience, not its.
For it, it is no different from falling on anything else,
With no assurance that it has finished falling
Or that it is falling still.
The window has a wonderful view of the lake,
But the view doesn't view itself.
It exists in this world
Colorless, shapeless, soundless, odorless and painless.

The lake's floor exists floorlessly,
And its shore exists shorelessly.
Its water feels itself neither wet nor dry,
And its waves to themselves are neither singular nor plural.
They splash deaf to their own noise
On pebbles neither large nor small;
And all this beneath a sky by nature skyless
In which the sun sets without setting at all
And hides without hiding behind an unminding cloud.
The wind ruffles it, its only reason being that it blows.
A second passes.
A second second.
A third.
But they are three seconds only to us.
Time has passed like a courier with urgent news,
But that's just our simile.
The character is invented,
His haste is make-believe,
His news inhuman.

by Wislawa Syzborska

7

Suffering in the Jungle

At the end of my 15-month stay at the retreat center, as the second 3-month silent retreat came to an end, I spoke with several teachers about my continued enthusiasm for, and belief in, the process of meditation as a path to freedom. Several encouraged me to take on the robes of a Buddhist monk in Asia. With Burma in the clutches of a military junta and Sri Lankan Buddhism languishing unreformed, Thailand seemed the best place to go. One teacher, Ajahn Sucitto, recommended Wat Pah Nanachat, the International Forest Monastery in Northeast Thailand. It had an English abbot, followed traditional Theravada teachings, and everyone in the monastery spoke English.

When the 3-month retreat ended, Joan flew out to join me, and the two of us drove across the country to Albuquerque. From there we flew to Bangkok, Thailand. We wandered and gawked

The entrance sign at International Forest Monastery

The outer meditation sala

like tourists, spending several months exploring that amazing city, as well as taking side trips to Luang Prabang, Laos and Phnom Penh, Cambodia. We also spent a week touring the magnificent ruins at Angkor Wat.

While Joan visited a family friend in Bangkok, I visited several monasteries that were equipped to teach westerners. Finally, I spent several weeks at the International Forest Monastery, "Wat Pah Nanachat."

Monks joined the monastery from countries all over the world: the U.S., Canada, England, Australia, Germany, France, Norway, Sweden, Italy, Japan, Philippines, Brazil, Argentina, Mexico and many others. It was exhilarating practicing with such a wide variety of people, all joined by the common desire to quest for that which was most meaningful in life.

I had found my new home. Reconnecting with Joan, I told her I had found the place where I wanted to ordain as a monk. A little over two months later we parted, she back to Albuquerque and me to begin the steps towards ordination.

The monastery was around a mile long by about a half mile wide. The front of the monastery was dense multi-layered old growth jungle made up of enormous 60-foot bamboos, high trees of all kinds, some as tall as 180 feet, and a tangle of small bamboo thickets. Thick ropey vines tangled through it all.

The morning sweep, using brooms made in the nearby village

Near the entrance into the monastery was a large sheet metal roofed, open-sided building called a *sala*. Here the community of monks, the *Sangha*, chanted devotions in Pali, the ancient language closest

Resident lay supporters; I'm on the left with two Germans, a Thai and a New Zealander

to that used by the Buddha, ate their single meal of the day and practiced meditation. The tropical heat added an unrelenting intensity.

For several months, I lived in the monastery as a layman. Wearing a white pajama-like uniform, I supported the monks through various acts of service, in the process losing about sixty pounds with the hard work amidst the intense heat.

Finally, my commitment remaining unabated, I was ordained as an anagarika, or "pra kow," a white-robed postulant.

Postulant Ordination Chant

The household life is cramped and dusty,
The homeless life is free as air.
It is not easy, living the household life,
To live the fully-perfected holy life,
Purified and polished like a conch shell.
Thus, having shaved off my hair and beard,
May I don the white robes of the anagarika (postulant),
And go forth from the household life to homelessness,
In dependence on the Triple Gem

A white robed postulant
cleaning up after the meal

Carefully following the daily activities of monastery life, I was on probation pending agreement by the sangha that I could become a brown robed member of the community. This period lasted just eight weeks for me.

After memorizing the appropriate chanting and having a full complement of brown dyed clothing issued to me by the monk in charge of cloth, I was officially sworn in as a novice. I seamlessly slipped into the body of the community, becoming just another face at the end of the row of monks silently eating their meal.

After thirteen months as a novice, I was accepted into the sangha as a full-fledged monk or bhikkhu.

Intense renunciation came with what was called "the holy life." Any possible source of self-aggrandizement based on my former occupation, nationality, class, personal wealth, race, or any other source of social status was simply to disappear. My name was taken away, and I received a new one: Satimanto, a Pali word meaning "he who is mindful, heedful or aware."

Chanting

Ordination — my first day as a full-fledged monk

Renunciation I

Let go of:

Name, Wife, Parents, Family, Old Religion, Home, Money, Power, Career, Class, Nationality, Hair, Clothes, Shoes, Sex, Comfort, Youth, Likes, Dislikes, Preconceptions.

A good start.

This hut was my home for six months

I was assigned to a hut or place to sleep depending on the needs of the monastery. Of course, I lived alone: no wife or close companion was possible. I was 100% celibate. I even thought of myself as being non-sexual!

I was encouraged to completely forget about the world and leave all those who had been near and dear behind. One teacher told me about the parents of the head abbot of our lineage who visited the monastery over which he presided to pay respects to the senior monk, not knowing that their son had been the head abbot there for many years! To the abbot, they were just another couple paying respects. This was right attitude.

Instead of sleeping in bed, I slept on the floor, my robes serving double duty as my bedding. Instead of central heating and air conditioning, the windows of my hut had no glass and remained open to the world regardless of the temperature or the inclemency of the weather. Instead of hot and cold running water, I took a cold-water bath out of a bucket. The typical uniform of a lawyer, the suit, was eons away from my new uniform, a few rectangles of unconstructed cloth. Having given up my dozen pairs of shoes, each designed for a different activity, I owned a single pair of saffron-colored plastic flip-flops.

Instead of choosing the food I ate from grocery store shelves or a restaurant's menu, I opened my bowl to whatever the local villagers decided they wanted to offer me for my single meal of the day. Once I was offered a gecko, a local lizard, which later sat a bit queasily in my stomach.

I also was encouraged to fast. Once, I fasted for 44 days while practicing deep in the high-altitude western Thai jungle. Another time I ate only every third day for many months.

Walking on alms round in the early morning

Alms Round

There is the same
Slight turning and bowing forward
As when the priest offers
The Consecrated Body of Christ.
But here is offered only
The Emptiness of the alms bowl:
Cool, circular, hollow.
Parishioners offer up to this robed figure
The food that sustains
In this world.

Every two weeks I cut my hair with a razor. Thai monks even shave their eyebrows! I had no money; in fact, it was a confessable offense even to touch the stuff! If I needed a toiletry or some small item like a flashlight, I asked the monk in charge of supplies for it. What was available and considered appropriate for a junior monk to own was given to me. Otherwise, I did without.

Monks do everything by seniority. When we ate in the main *sala*, the head monk (abbot) ate seated at the top end of the line and, twenty monks away, the newest novice ate at the bottom end. As many privileges were distributed by seniority, I often did without or with less than other more senior monks. The comfort and convenience in entertaining likes and dislikes were not possible. I did as I was told and bowed for the honor.

Sandals

Deep cross-cracks are just starting at the sole
Matching mate already split edge to edge;
Arch straps cut off long ago
—too short for these swelling feet—
Replaced by floppy pack straps;
Heel straps glued, screwed and
Tied underneath for good measure;
Adjusting straps gone, sewn tightly
Just past worn out buckles.
Tattered ruins, yes,
But they still protect these feet
Crossing razor sharp ravines
In the rain.

Being a monk meant being entirely
dependent on lay people. They provided food, clothing, housing, and
transportation. They paid the light
bills and purchased tools for the shop
and sewing machines. When one saw
how well supplied the monastery was,
one could understand the devotion the
villagers felt for their religion. Just as
anywhere else, wealthy householders
boasted to the poorer members of the
village about how generous they were.

Food being offered by
lay supporters

Every so often, the practice would
continue in a different place. Once I
lived for about four months in a cave high above the Mekong River,
walking down each morning at first light to a tiny fishing village
for alms round. The geography of the monastery, also a National
Park, was like a wet version of Southeast Utah, an exotic black
sandstone world of potholes and smoothly sculpted mountain
shoulders. Above my cave, there were miles of high cliffs with
views into Laos. Very few people visited.

My cave perched high on a cliff edge above the Mekong

Wild

A long time now I've been living wild,
Silently begging food each morning
In the little fishing village
On the banks of the great river
Far below this cliff aerie cave.
Meditating — sitting and walking —
I live roofless below the cliff swallow's nest.
Bathing in a great round rock crystalline basin,
Wind-etched wood forms a simple Buddha shrine.
In this glade of low trees beneath the sky,
Simple squares of cloth washed close
By schools of tiny fish.
Walking, the robes covering the body
Flap crazy rhythms in the wild wind.
Vaulted above is the high star dome
With Milky Way stripe,
While I crouch here below on
On this flowing sandstone precipice edge.
Barest light breaks on
Far Lao mountain peaks.
These eyes are sharp and alert,
Like gray-specked neighbor hawk,
But with no will to hunt, just
Soft, Open, Vulnerable,
Sweeping this great floating world
With loving-kindness,
Nothing in everything,
Emptiness in the palm of infinite possibility,
Wildness in the heart.

The cave was a rock roof vaulted gallery at the top of a great broken rock face was on the Thai side of the Mekong river. It had a sweeping view of that great river, and just out of view was the tiny fishing village far below that fed me each morning.

Darkness

In this flickering candlelight,
I think maybe 30,000 termites
Cross my robe tonight
Across the bamboo drying rod
Notched 'tween two slabs of rock
In this cave
Suspended between the precipice and
Rain-swollen Mekong below.

Six feet away —
Eating, sleeping, and meditation occur.
On this split bamboo platform
Sitting in four oil-filled cans,
An island amidst a sea of insect tusks
Rustling all around in the night.

I know how to expertly pee
Into an old Pepsi bottle,
Not a drop is spilled.
Rolling back down,
A vertebra pops quietly
Back to the sitting cushion,
Now a pillow.

Once there was a festival in the village, and I walked through crowds of merrymakers and booths filled with smells and color. That day I got a beautiful chicken breast to eat — complete with an elegant claw! Another time, it was the Queen's birthday, and the bowl filled quickly with a hundred Oreo cookies! The regular fare was sticky rice, an easily eaten nutritious food with a mild, nutty taste.

Chant

During the Rains Retreat
Sitting and walking here in the cave;
An octave above
And sometimes interwoven with
The smooth thrumming of
The great Mekong sliding by
The sound of group chanting
In an unknown language.

Another time I lived for several months on a tiny platform the size of a double bed in dense, leech infested high altitude jungle atop the rugged ridgeline dividing Thailand and Burma (Myanmar). Screaming gibbons swung through the tree tops high above me while a camera hidden by lay supporters recorded boars, tigers and bears passing near my campsite.

The leeches were especially taxing. As I walked down the main trail, I could see all around me little two-inch-long black funnel-shaped leeches quivering with the knowledge of my approach. As I came within a few meters, they would start inch-worming towards me. If I stopped for just a few seconds, they would begin to climb up my unprotected flesh. Bucket baths became mad as I stood on a plastic square, racing the leeches to complete my wash!

During my stay there I fasted for 45 days (I had a bit of powdered milk and a few sugar cubes each day) and did not come away from my little perch for 50 days. My mind became incredibly light and pure.

Standing in a swirl of butterflies,
Sun flashes,
Giant bamboo twists and shouts:
Wind roars
Hello!

During one all night sit with the other monks in the main hall out at the end of a stone headland sticking out and above its rocky surrounds, the jungle all around burned. Illegal loggers wanted us to leave, and this was their less than subtle way of expressing their desires. But the fires slowly were banked by a gentle mist.

At the end of that first searing year in the robes, Joan wrote that she wished "closure" to our relationship and asked for a divorce. Never had I imagined receiving such a letter! I wrote her back, saying clearly that I did not want a divorce, but I felt I could not oppose her wishes since I was not carrying out the responsibilities of a husband. I wrote in dismay to my mother-in-law, telling her this news. She matter-of-factly replied that Joan and I had been growing apart for years and that the news did not surprise her. Now I was even more shocked! I felt that my love for Joan remained vigorous and steady, despite my far-flung spiritual odyssey. She had supported me throughout. Now, a simple "I need you, please come home" would probably have sufficed to make me re-engage with her on a deeper level, but no such open-hearted exchange took place.

I now understood that Joan was not happy about my desire to be a monk, but I did not want to end our relationship with a divorce. But I also knew that such an attitude was unfair if my partner did not appreciate our newly attenuated relationship sufficiently to wait. At an impasse, I acquiesced to her desire. I signed the formal papers about a year later. A sense of profound sadness enveloped me, and for years I deeply grieved her loss. I called it my "love divorce."

Good-bye

Gray clouds
Trees vibrate GREEN!
Loving you
Makes me a perpetual exile.
Rain pelting down cats and dogs
Embracing this lonely old fool.

My yearning for spiritual meaning had trumped any other commitment. I yearned for wisdom, and I was willing to give up everything to find it. She assumed there was no place anymore for her in my world. From her perspective years later, she told me that she simply respected my wishes to practice as a monk and therefore turned away to get on with her life. Never had I realized how different our life strategies were. As I followed my passionate dreams toward monastic life, she headed towards a life of calm reason and logic. The loss of Joan was a painful, heart-wrenching price that I felt I had to pay to practice. Never had I felt so alone.

Circle Game

Walking the little path by the hut,
Turning and starting over again — and again
Beneath the two old mango trees,
This aging peacock aspires to be a
Wild snow goose,
Dreaming of high mountain ridge shoulders.
Lust gone for now and no ill-will felt,
Only my old friend confusion keeps me stable.
Now coming back to the sitting mat —
There's even less to call "me" in
This sweaty dream world!

8

Monastic Life

The only community that mattered to me on a day to day basis was the community of other beings in brown robes and those lay supporters who offered me food. I saw a few white clad lay people from a distance at the meal, but only for a few minutes each day, except for the weekly all night sit. The rest of the time was taken up with the concerns of my fellow monastics.

One of our most intimate contacts with the villagers was a sober viewing of the bodies of their dead loved ones just before they were to be burned in the monastery's small crematorium.

The daily schedule was simple and relentlessly repetitive. After a four to six-hour sleep on the wooden floor of the hut, the day began with

the 3 a.m. bell. I volunteered for the job of ringing the bell for about six months.

Rising at 2:30, I climbed the ladder up into the dark bell tower and lit a tiny candle, selecting one of the large wooden mallets stored there. I then rang the bell in a very precise pattern, starting with very quick little taps, and finally smacking it in a slow cadence with all my strength. The bell itself was the casing from a Vietnam era unexploded 500-pound bomb. It had a beautiful, mellow tone that carried across the paddies to the little villages that surrounded the monastery grounds.

At 3 am the monks came together for half an hour of devotional chanting, sitting on thin mats on the cement floor of the huge *sala*. This was followed by an hour of silent meditation. Three large Buddha images, each covered in gold leaf and filled with gifts of melted gold jewelry and precious jewels, towered above us. During other periods of the year, we practiced alone in our huts, silently following the breath as it moved like ocean waves in and out of the body.

Meal setup was at 5 am. We each brought our covered steel bowl to our eating spot. The bowl was about a foot in diameter, encased in brown knit yarn to which was attached a long shoulder strap. I placed the bowl at my place along the 4-foot-wide cement shelf that extended along one whole side of the sala. Next, I lay out my square sitting cloth, placing a spittoon for waste, a few simple utensils, and my steel cup beside it.

Once this simple task was complete and dawn had officially occurred, the alms round began. Assigned to one of 5 different routes, I put on both my outer robes and now swaddled in some 15 yards of material, but with my feet bare, I placed my bowl strap around my neck and silently padded out of the monastery. This was the only time in the day I usually was allowed to leave the monastery.

It was a very special time of day. In the cool, early morning light my bare feet slapped the pavement, gravel, or soft soil of the outside world, as

our little row of monks walked between three and six miles. We followed a precise route. Along the road, villagers kneeled as we approached. First, they held their palms together in reverent greeting. Then they pulled a fistful of sticky rice out of traditional bamboo leaf containers and placed it in our bowl, sometimes including other foods like unrefrigerated eggs, noodles, or little plastic bags of curry or desserts.

An atmosphere of reverence permeated the ritual. Sometimes villagers bowed three times after completing this exercise of generosity. Through their unforced generosity, the whole lifestyle of a monk was possible. Sometimes villagers offered monks expensive delicacies that they could not afford to feed their children. I naturally had deep gratitude for our community of supporters. And so I was nourished.

During the early years, I ate "*dok bot*" almost every day, mainly a combination of whatever was offered and placed in the bowl by the community. This was a particular ascetic or "*dhutanga*" practice, one of thirteen recommended by the Buddha, which required only eating what was given by others.

The 13 Dhutanga Practices

1. Wearing patched or mended robes.
2. Wearing only the three robes and no others.
3. Receiving alms food on alms round.
4. Not omitting any house on the alms round.
5. Eating only once a day, at one sitting.
6. Eating only out of the alms bowl.
7. Eating to satiety, refusing further food.
8. Living in the forest.
9. Living under a tree.
10. Living in the open, not at the foot of a tree or under a roof.
11. Living in a charnel ground (a place where bodies are burned).
12. Being satisfied with any bed or resting place.
13. Never lying down, always sitting.

On such a day, after returning to the monastery and washing my sore feet, I de-packaged everything, placed it on the sticky rice and poured a thermos of boiled water over it all. This was my single meal for the day.

Returning to the main *sala*, we sat silently by our bowls, listening to a short talk in Thai given by the abbot to the lay people before the meal. Then all the monks chanted an ancient blessing

to those who offered food
for that day's meal and the
laity moved off to eat whatever was left over from alms
round. The head monk rang
a little bell, and all the monks
fervently absorbed them-
selves in taste sensation. It
was an excellent practice to
minimize this time, so I often
ate in ten to fifteen minutes.
Twenty-five minutes later,
the bell rang again, and we
put down our spoons. The
meal was over.

Next was bowl cleanup. I
set my bowl on a small rubber ring on the forest floor
and dished plastic bowlfuls
of soapy water out of a great
clay cistern, washing and rinsing the
bowl, cup, and spoon. Then I returned
to my hut or *kuti*, set the bowl in the sun
to dry, hung up the washing clothes and
then changed into work robes.

For a long time, I was the cloth
monk, assigned to the sewing *kuti*. I
organized the monastery's supply of
robes, bathing clothes, meal clothes,
etc. I sewed new robes for novices
and dyed them by soaking them in a boiling tea made from
wood chips laboriously chopped from a native tree. I also sewed
new robes for newly arriving white-robed postulants, offering

these as gifts to those taking the first step on the road to becoming a monk.

After a few hours of work, I returned to my hut. There I might take a short nap or read. But most of the remainder of the day was spent in sitting and walking meditation, about an hour of sitting in meditation posture followed by an hour of contemplative walking. This was done very slowly, a controlled, relaxed movement back and forth along a section of path about thirty paces long.

Teatime, a welcome diversion, arrived about 4:30 in the afternoon. We assembled and drank two cups of tea, coffee or cocoa along with a few candies or pieces of chocolate. After tea, there was more sitting and walking meditation. This was the rhythm of my average day.

There were also weekly rhythms to the monastic life. Every quarter moon there was an all-night sit. The full-fledged monks gathered and exchanged confessions for the offenses committed during the previous two weeks. These might include intentionally slapping an insect or breaking a twig while walking through the jungle. Many of the offenses confessed gave refined attention to non-violence. Stopping the cycle of birth and death was what monastic practice was all about. A monk's training aimed at non-action, or if action was necessary, an action generating only minimal or neutral karmic consequences. That's why we confessed acts which produced adverse effects in the world. More severe offenses had to be brought before the whole community immediately after they had been committed.

Meeting on these special full and new moon nights in the small ordination hall, we sat in a formal arrangement based on seniority. Stiff in full meditation posture, we listened to the recitation of the Patimokkha, the 227 basic rules of a monk. This was done in the Pali language, the language closest to the spoken word of the Buddha. The complete recitation took about 45 minutes.

Patimokkha

After these many lawyer years
Representing the thousands charged before the Tribunal
Despite an idealistic naivete that sticks to this old bird like glue,
I am intimate with the ways of the world.
Yes, and weary too.

Sitting forearms length from
These brown robed practitioners,
Back held straight in formal meditation pose,
The ancient Code is from memory recited:
Sacred Icon, most ancient talisman,
Ode to purity and self-respect!

I know unshakably:
Here there is a sense of shame,
Great guardian of the world;
Here there is sensed
Danger in the slightest fault.

The sure knowledge of this gives a
Sense of bold security:
These are good, even noble men,
True brothers, fellow oarsmen for
Crossing the flood of the senses!

After the recitation, the novices and postulants joined the monks. These junior monastics chanted similar but much shorter verses of confession and recommitment to their rules. Then we listened to a talk by the head monk, often about disciplinary matters. Traditionally, a night of meditation practice followed.

Many monks did not stay up the whole night during "monk's day," but I made it a point to do so. During the wee hours of the morning, I would stagger back and forth like some old drunk for hours at a time on a short path.

I became addicted to the cleansing effect sleep deprivation had on me. The next morning, I would feel serene and mild, the mind light. It seemed easier to let go of ingrained behavior and speech patterns on that day.

Then there were the seasonal rhythms. During the hot season, I sat quietly in my hut and watched the sweat beading and dripping off the body. Any heavier work like hauling firewood involved wearing totally soaked, sweat drenched robes for hours.

The rainy season cooled the earth somewhat. All kinds of unusual forms of wriggling, slithering and hopping life showed themselves during these days of relentless rain. The paddies became a vibrant emerald green as rice, the lifeblood to both the villagers and the monks, grew tall on sturdy stalks.

This was the time of most intensive and sequestered practice by the monks. Rice harvest time coincided with the end of the annual 3-month intensive meditation retreat, followed by a Thanksgiving-like series of celebrations.

Then came the cold season. Sixty degrees Fahrenheit was as cold as it got, but with no shoes, socks, underwear, or any fitted clothes, it felt quite cold. We wore sleeveless tubes of thick wool like sweater vests for these cooler temperatures, although I still shivered. These went under the standard thin cotton sashes we wore over the left shoulder, always keeping the right shoulder respectfully bare when in the monastery. Only when we left the monastery did we cover the right shoulder.

Finally, there was the great cycle of a single lifetime for a monk. As one entered the monastery, one spent up to a year as a white-robed postulant, adapting to the monastic schedule and taking care of the monks by doing hundreds of mundane chores or simple services, many of them simple cleaning. Next one graduated to brown robes and took on the vows of a novice. This period also lasted about one year. Here the novice was educated about his responsibilities and slowly attuned to the moral standards of a full-fledged monk.

9

Just Sitting

For we must view this fleeting world,
A star at dawn,
A bubble in a stream,
A flash of lightning in a summer sky,
A flickering lamp,
A phantom
And a dream.

Diamond Sutra

Months became years. The internal changes took place, both subterranean and systemic. Abilities to pinpoint or otherwise describe these changes — when they birthed and how they matured — became difficult. But however it happened, the consequences of living a life of restraint and renunciation seeped into consciousness. And I was profoundly changed.

Conditions inside the monastery tended to encourage the higher mind: compassion, generosity, virtue, concentration and contemplation. The passions which ruled the world outside — money, power, sexual attraction and its ubiquitous commercial manipulation of greed, hatred, and fear — were distractions often minimized.

Visitors sometimes could not understand that differences between the worlds on the two sides of the monastery's walls were more apparent than real. The world was as much alive inside the monastery as it was outside in the city. Regardless of our individual practices, the competition between monks was evident in the quest for power, knowledge, and status, however refined.

Of course, we all looked to the other monks as models to deepen our practices. To my untrained eye, some of the junior monks seemed arrogant, self-centered, and overly confident of the subtleties of Buddhist dogma, while a few others were remarkable people. It seemed to me that new seekers coming to the monastery came in two flavors: those motivated from the head and those driven from the heart. I thought those who were intellectually attracted to the elegance of Buddhist psychology, philosophy, and cosmology seemed to be the ones most susceptible to grandiose visions of themselves. I was one of these. I was quite familiar with these motivations and well aware of my own grandiosity.

I saw myself in the other group as well, those sad ones with aching hearts, those who came to the monastery battered and bruised by the world. They understood the futility and meaninglessness of life when lived without spiritual purpose or direction. And while I certainly was intellectually attracted to Buddhism, I came primarily to heal a heart made sick by the futility of life itself.

I also observed that as one looked up the line towards the increasingly senior monks, one saw more of the fruits of the spiritual life. Senior monks tended to be mild mannered, unassuming, integrated, peaceful — and spiritually powerful — people. They were easy to respect. So of course, I wanted this for myself.

Senior monks taught that a critical component of practice, especially in the first few years, was patient endurance. Junior monks like me disliked the severe living conditions and claustrophobic lack of freedoms. But distress arising from these perceptions was primary grist for practice.

So, life happened. The practice had an intense, immediate physical impact, living as I was in the jungle with its wild animals, poisonous snakes and insects, sleeping on wooden boards, and patiently suffering as the heat and cold of days and seasons passed.

In the early years, the monastery appeared to me to be a cross between a Marine Corps boot camp and a Boy Scout jamboree. Most of the daily activities of the postulants, novices, and junior monks involved hard work — sweeping, cleaning, constructing, digging, sewing and washing. Every element of the daily routine such as alms round, the meal and keeping robes and huts clean took considerable amounts of time. It seemed like there was precious little time for sitting and walking practice and little or no control over what one did or when one did it.

Lots of time was spent on taking care of the mundane needs of the more senior monks. Many acts of submission were required. Bowing to Buddha images and senior monks happened many times each day. The focus was on serving others in a very direct, physical way without thought or complaint, always cultivating the ability to give up control over every facet of life. This is how one prospered as a junior monk.

"Submersion of the self" required a personal discipline sufficient to win an ongoing internal war. It involved a strange kind of "pulling oneself up by one's bootstraps." In other words, I used my will and my discipline to overcome my willfulness, to believe a narrative that did *not* include believing my own stories. To survive in monastic life, I injected meaning into what were otherwise meaningless repetitions. Bringing meaning to these acts required faith in the Buddha's "recipe" for the path, faith in that which was beyond knowing. I realized that belief — faith — was an indispensable source for the practice — and for life itself.

Moving ever so slowly —
Sensation floods this consciousness as
Ankles, knees, and thighs are
Peeled from meditation posture lock.
Rotating on this sore hip to
Climb off sitting platform to
Shuffle off to
Walking meditation path;
Slowly mind settles in to
Stiff feet half a century old.

One of the chief differences between secularized Western Buddhist meditation as practiced in the States and ancient Asian Buddhist monasticism was the relative importance given to devotion. Western meditation teachers often emphasized the scientific or psychological nature of what was taking place during meditation. They invited the practitioner to "come and see" the benefits of the practice. Thus, liberation resulted from reliance on one's own scientifically based efforts. The Western Buddhist practitioner could, and often did, remain in control. This emphasis appealed to those who had rejected the irrational qualities emphasized in the Judeo-Christian tradition.

In contrast to this "scientific" perspective, Asian Buddhist monastic practice focused on faith in and devotion towards the

Buddha and senior monks. One example was chanting. Chanting filled a major role in the cycle of each day. Many hours were spent memorizing dozens of different chants, all in Pali. While it was possible to find poor English translations of the chants, learning their literal meaning was not emphasized. Mere repetition of these sounds, chanted by monks for over a hundred generations, was said to bring progress on the path to liberation. Faith in the Buddha's teaching was the ultimate mental result of chanting. Increasingly, I understood that faith was an essential element of the path.

As the length of time I imagined it took to reach liberation lengthened from a several years to lifetimes, I realized I had to have faith in the efficacy of the practice beyond any physical evidence. I had to implicitly trust the Buddhist scriptures to carry out their directions in daily practice. When the endless cycles of sitting and walking meditation became too dry to bear, I "moistened" meditation by chanting. Cultivating devotion — faith — made the practice come alive again.

And through it all, the profound language of monastic life with its endless repetitions had begun its work on my heart. Very slowly these immediate physical experiences grew stronger than my internal chatter. It seemed that my internal chatter just ran out of things to chat about after a while. The monk's routine, stripped of its novelty by repetition, became the norm, no longer unreasonable or difficult. It was just the way things were. I observed as a simple, childlike faith grew in my heart.

Similarly, in my contemplations, I realized that grace was an essential part of Buddhist practice. While the general evolution of the practice could be described, each monk's experience was unique, a bestowal of unmerited favor. Some monks thrived while others left the practice defeated. There was much I could do, at least initially, but success was beyond my power to "achieve." Ultimately, I had to die to the idea of being able to control anything truly important.

I could desire peace until I was blue in the face, but I could not attain it without letting go of that desire, indeed without dying to all desire. Liberation was beyond wanting, beyond controlling, a gift from the ineffable laws of "the way things were." I could cultivate the path like a farmer cultivated his fields, knowing nothing about the miraculous cycles of growth and decline, rain and drought, but simply trusting that harvest time would come. Just faith and grace, endlessly repeated. Here is where I found peace, in faith beyond my ability to conceptualize or comprehend, beyond my ability to even actualize.

Contemplating the power of this child-like faith brought me face to face with my old childhood version of Christianity. Now I could hold the old Christiana tenets close enough to my heart to experience reverence and devotion towards them without having to understand them intellectually. Faith had become a habit. Physical, emotional and mental ease grew from right here. Now, these were the norm rather than some peak experience. Practices at first forced, became habitual.

I eased back and relaxed, enjoying being alive and present in the moment. There was a natural ability to allow inside whatever was happening, not to change it or control it. Life was simple and easy.

Good-bye

River slides by far below this precipice;
A single, spare drift of rain caresses the face;
A slow, swelling glow advances across distant hills
Birthing out this new day!

Multitudes of cloud tracery
Filigree the entire sky!
Crystalline crimson, peach, orange,
Cream, and azure blue
Fill the full vault edge to edge.

In the midst of all this ease, of course, things changed. Suddenly, I found myself beset by new intensities of again wanting an intimate relationship with my wife. Confession during the weekly Pattimokkha failed to stem the longing coursing through my body and mind. Finally, engaging in a period of public penitence showed to those around me that I was not a perfect monk and accentuated the truth that such a goal was impossible.

Slowly, as the months passed, the crisis eased and I relaxed even more. I continued to fast by eating every third day to create a quieter space to practice, partly due to my frustration with how arduous it was to prepare for the meal. Sometimes, following the ancient rituals took as much as four hours just to complete a five-minute meal! I began to chafe at the rituals required in Thailand because I greatly enjoyed the solitude.

But I also found new respect for Christian teachings that taught that the sacred was inextricably mixed with the profane in daily life. Instead of battling my celibacy, I wondered if I could integrate it as a part of a spiritual path out in the world of household life. Perhaps a change in attitude could turn a powerful hindrance into a beautiful force for good. Could it be possible that sexuality could lift me up rather than drag me down? And with that thought came an immediate, powerful yearning for a family, a wife and children. Then that too passed.

After three and a half years in Thailand, I learned of an English monk of great learning and spiritual depth who ran a monastery in

Ajahn Brahmavamso,
my Australian abbot

our lineage near Perth, on the southwest coast of Australia. Getting my abbot's permission, I wrote the Australian monastery asking for permission to visit there.

With permission in hand, I left Thailand and traveled to a different world — Western Australia. Despite being far more austere than the state prison down the road, the first impression was of luxury. Showers! No bugs! Clothing! Shoes! The monastery provided clothing that was warm and dry. The huts were weatherproof, and the walking paths were covered to protect from rain. Instead of meditation practice on cement or tiles, the nearly new Australian monastery offered thickly padded carpeting in a simple, beautiful meditation hall. There were very few group activities and great latitude in how one spent one's days. My woodworking skills were greatly appreciated and put to good use on many interesting, challenging wood projects, and these brought enthusiastic thanks from the senior monks. Life here was a breeze after Thailand.

In mid-2004, the relative ease of monastic life in Australia was punctuated by serious illness. First, I contracted a vicious case of pneumonia which required hospitalization for five days. But instead of a quick recovery after release from the hospital, I continued to weaken. I could breathe, but it did not seem to help. Just the slightest exercise caused exhaustion, leaving me on my hands and knees panting. I was at a loss as to how to proceed. I just watched and waited.

After ten days of this, I lost consciousness while washing my bowl and eventually I was rushed to the hospital. The doctors there told me I had a saddle embolism, a clot blocking both main blood passages from the heart to the lungs. One doctor said that this was often a fatal condition. The part of the heart that pumped blood to the lungs was greatly constricted by the blockage, so there was tachycardia, the heart racing away at 120 or more beats per minute. I could send my heart rate soaring to 180 just by lifting my hand!

The doctors remained unsure as to the cause but thought that deep venal thrombosis (clots from the lower legs from sitting meditation) and schistosomiasis (water borne blood flukes I picked up years before while living by the Mekong River) were the likely causes. There was nothing to be done but start me on blood thinning medication and wait for my antibodies to destroy the clot. I spent eleven more days in the hospital slowly regaining my strength, followed by several months doing little around the monastery.

It was a powerful experience. In my considerably weakened state, I contemplated my mortality in a more immediate way than ever before. There was nothing of importance to do here on earth anymore, that was true. On the other side of death, another life loomed. Clarifying the mind all the way to liberation could very well take more than one lifetime to accomplish. In the end, there was nothing else for it but to continue. Returning to the world involved returning to the same shackles on the mind. And so, I resolved that such an alternative was unthinkable.

The whole world is on fire, I tell you!
It's blazing, blazing!
The whole world's aflame—
Flaring, shaking,
The whole world rocks.
Even these words are shaking—
The whole world's ablaze!

Elder Nun Susapacola, Thig. 202-3

I greatly enjoyed the Australian monastery and wanted to stay, but I was unable to extend my temporary Australian visa despite an invitation from the head monk to remain. Because of my weakened physical condition, he advised me to stay close to a good quality western health system, and after some vacillation, I decided to return to America. The day my year-long Australian visa lapsed, I flew to the single American monastery in our lineage, located about two hours north of San Francisco in the beautiful northern California wine country near Ukiah.

The environment here was even worldlier than in Australia. Monks regularly worked in the well-equipped office. I worked on the website and re-organized the digital and hard-copy libraries. I spent hours copying "Dhamma talks" by the senior monks onto hundreds of CDs. The food was excellent, and the tidy glass-enclosed huts scattered over the steep little valley afforded comfortable, often scenic places for practice.

I read everything. Where in earlier years I had restricted my reading to Buddhist scripture and books authored by members of our direct lineage, now I ranged widely, reading history, biography, psychology, popular science, even novels. While conditions were still relatively Spartan, they were luxurious compared to Asian standards. Enthusiasm for the monastic life slowly was replaced by a feeling that I was just motoring along, marking time.

I had arrived at the bedrock of who I was, but all the doing, all the not doing, still left me here in this body, listening to this breath. The recent severe illness made it clear that time was short and a sense of spiritual urgency remained unabated.

10

Presence

Trained as I was in traditional Asian Buddhist practices, strong opinions about what a monk's life should look like conflicted with the new environment. These views had to change if I was to appreciate California.

It felt great to be back in America, but the variety of comforts and other things common to Western culture seemed, well, overdone. Monks regularly used computers, burned CDs, printed documents and used telephones. Many monks sent emails and used the internet recreationally, although it was heavily filtered to avoid contact with sexual content. A lot of chatting between the monks went on as well. And it appeared to me that the line between laity and monk had grown thin indeed.

Arriving at the monastery in midsummer, I was invited to attend a family get-together in Memphis in late November 2005 to celebrate my sister Mary's and my joint birthdays. It was the first time I had been out of a monastery for more than a few hours since my illness in September and October of 2004 and the first time I had seen some members of my family in almost eight years.

During the time spent abroad, I had only received a few letters, friendly but primarily not understanding what I was doing.

For several decades, our family had come together for reunions about once every five years, but other than those meetings, we lived quite separate lives.

Nevertheless, I enjoyed a special relationship with my brothers and sisters. As a family, we had experienced unusual upbringings that had shaped us in unique ways. As a result, all of us were in some form or another outside the mainstream. We all thought of ourselves as being special and unique — members of a strange fraternity. While we lived strikingly different lives- and lived widely dispersed across America, we also shared deep bonds.

When I arrived, my entire family was lined up at the airport to greet me. I had grown used to not being touched except by medical practitioners. Now I was the target of vigorous hugs by my brothers John and Dave, my brother-in-law Henry, my nephew Jonathon, my sisters Mary and Connie and finally by my sisters-in-law Janet and Pat. Each of them seemed genuine in their expressions of love for me. I had warned them that I could not be touched by females due to the rules of the monastic form, but the women of my family went right ahead anyway. My embarrassment was only matched by the depth of my feelings of connection with them all. It was a lovely and profound moment, water to a thirsty man.

But the week with my family was disorienting. The peace and connection I felt in my heart jarred with my environment as I silently paced through the early hours of the morning in my brother's lavishly furnished French country style home. I felt at ease and warmly connected to my family through our lifelong bonds of kinship and shared experience. At the same time, I felt like a visitor from Mars in this unfamiliar environment. There were upholstered chairs to sit on, food available at any time, colorful clothing, sounds of music and television, constant conversation, and many recreational opportunities. I felt uneasy and out of place.

All my siblings were lifelong Christians. For years, I had judged them to be running away from their problems, denying the possibility of insight by superstitiously hiding in the folds of Jesus' robes. But my experience that week contrasted starkly with that old image. All of them had practiced daily devotions and prayer throughout their lives. While we shared our memories, both old and new, I realized that each of them in their way was showing the fruits of their spiritual practice. Our collective intimacy was a beautiful experience for me. I espe-

Meditating in
Alaska at Mary's

cially enjoyed our silly celebrations around eldest brother Dave's upcoming retirement.

I had always believed that I was the black sheep of my family, although my siblings disagreed. During previous times with my family, I had felt alienated, outside the family circle. Lost in my arrogance, I had interpreted this as indicative of my superior depth and wisdom. I was simply in a different league.

But this time my attitude contrasted sharply with those old, arrogant imaginings. Now I felt like I was talking to my closest friends, exchanging feelings and experiences that were close to my heart with ease and mutual understanding. There were several intimate moments with my family, and our spiritual common ground shook the foundations of my antipathy towards Christianity.

I was especially moved to hear about the large numbers of people who had been praying for me. Some, like my siblings, had prayed daily on my behalf for 40 years! Dozens of people had set aside times of fasting and prayer, focusing their spiritual intentions for my benefit.

I joined the family at church that Sunday. What an experience! There I was in my brown robes, surrounded by people singing praise music at the top of their lungs, their hands up in the air in what looked like some Nazi salute! Everything was tightly choreographed so not a second of "dead" time occurred between the various sections of the service. I worried that all this emotionalism, once aroused, could be manipulated by those church leaders controlled by greed or lust for power.

Despite these jarring elements, I enjoyed the service. I interpreted it from the perspective of thinking that all those around me were coming to this experience with goodwill and with good intentions. The sermon, drawn from Ecclesiastes, was especially interesting. Here, King Solomon wrote this book of the Bible from his opulent palace. In it, he saw through all the so-called successes of the world, describing them as meaningless, as mere vanity, as "dust in the wind." Having penetrated to this profound insight — that God had given all according to His inscrutable will, and that someday all would be taken away — Solomon wrote that there was nothing worth doing other than to revere God and to live life fully through the honoring of the ancient ethical disciplines.

That day I read the whole book. From my Buddhist practice, I knew that human effort focused on advancement in this world was futile, so the message of Ecclesiastes resonated deeply in my heart. Suddenly there was a kinship, a bridge between my beliefs and my Bible loving family. And indeed, their love for me was softening and touching my lonely heart.

My interest piqued, I asked my oldest brother Dave if he would be willing to give me a Bible. He immediately handed over his family Bible, covered with 40 years of notes and filled with his personal records. I was shocked! Of course, I couldn't take something from him that was as profoundly valuable as this, the centerpiece of his family's daily devotions! I declined.

Later I realized that the experience had left me with a visceral feeling of unworthiness. I did not deserve such a gift, such sacrifice from my brother. I remembered the lump in my throat as I remembered his enthusiasm in letting go of this most sacred of his possessions.

I became eager to study the Bible! I had always argued that the Bible was just another book, written by people like you and me. But

My family: Mary, David, John, Connie and myself

then I recalled my attitude towards the Buddhist monks' "requisites," his bowl and robes.

I came to believe that these simple physical items were imbued with a sacred quality, that there was something in them that bespoke of holiness. Now I was beginning to think of the Bible in a similar way. I accepted the belief that it was a sacred book, written by godly men inspired by the Holy Spirit. I understood what it meant to live Christ into the world as these Bible writers had done. It was more than just another document. The belief grew in me that the Bible was worthy of my closest attention.

After the reunion, I returned to the monastery changed. I spent many hours contemplating what had happened. I had always cherished Christian ethics even while rejecting the traditional Christianity I knew from childhood. Throughout my life, I had seen Christ's words in the Bible as a powerful model for how one was to live in the world. I easily respected people who called themselves Christians, even when their behavior did not seem to warrant respect. Now, wrapped in my Buddhist robes, sequestered away behind the walls of my monastery, I silently contemplated this shift in the heart.

When I left Christianity in my early teens, I had imagined my reasons to be intellectual. It was only now, four decades later, that I saw the anger, fear and emotional hurt beneath those rationalizations. Now I saw these as the real fuel for my intellectual dissent. Pacing the walking path outside my forest hut, garbed in the brown robes of a Buddhist monk, I began to reassess the Christianity of my youth.

I had toughed it through the most difficult years of monastic practice. The attrition rate was high for everyone throughout the early periods of practice, but for the Americans who began the practice in Asia, few survived. One rule of thumb was that half of all who started each stage of practice dropped out before its end: half of the beginning white-robed postulants left, half of the one-year novices left, half of the early year full-fledged monks, etc.

I had survived. Part of it was just that I was a stubborn cuss, but also, I genuinely believed in what I was doing. Now, my convictions in the rightness of the choices I had made in taking the monastic path shook. There was a shift in my core values, from "resting in emptiness" to faith seeking relationship, especially in turning towards praise and worship of that which was beyond. I began to see something like a personal God out there.

I also yearned to use my hands and heart to serve. I spent some time talking with a pastor during the reunion, laying out very honestly what was going on. He was familiar with my family and my personal history, and I trusted his integrity and honesty. He ended our interview by just posing a simple question: "What are you doing for children now?"

A few months later, my eldest brother Dave died. He got up in the middle of the night to go to the bathroom, something broke inside and massive internal bleeding led to his death only a few hours later. At the family reunion, he had talked about his readiness to leave this world and go to the Father. Now, as he had put it then, he had indeed "graduated."

Again, our family came together. Carrying his ashes up the highest mountain in Georgia, we shared memories, poems, and stories about our lives with Dave. At the summit, we scattered his ashes to the four winds. I threw his titanium hip joint into the air off the top of the mountain and watched it spin into the distant brush. All of us were pulled together by this unexpected grief. His death cut into my heart in a new way and left me with a deep, visceral understanding of the fragility of life. How quickly we come and go on this Earth!

I asked for a Bible from my brother, John. Finally, he sent me one. Carrying the exquisitely bound book out to my tiny hut in the northern California forest, I sat down and opened it at random. Thus began a series of compelling experiences. These experiences seemed to come from a place beyond me and my adult choices. They were unexpected and mysterious. As I read, a sense of liquid joy poured over me like a waterfall. It was almost too much to bear. It overloaded my senses. In response, surging joy came from the depths of my heart and poured out into the world.

I felt an overwhelming loving presence, accepting me, inviting me and engaging me out of a mysterious well of pure love. Old feelings of trusting faith in the Buddha's teachings gave way to a very different intention, to a passionate demand for a direct relationship with Christ. Tears streaked down my cheeks.

Again and again, a sense of loving presence overwhelmed everything else. Forces beyond my control or understanding moved me. I contacted a world of intense joy, and Christ unfurled in my heart.

My sisters in Alaska organized a reunion during the coming summer. My sister Connie, her three children and their families had settled in Fairbanks. Because of their geographic isolation, I hadn't seen them for many years, and some I had never met. My sister Mary, marrying the patriarch of a large extended family also based in Fairbanks, moved there as well. There were many new faces to meet in Alaska.

I spent two weeks in Fairbanks, the first week simply with my sister, Mary. That week proved to be a potent time for me. I devoured the Bible, finding particular pleasure in reading Eugene Peterson's Bible paraphrase, "The Message." I read for hours at a time, feeling a keen resonance with what I was taking in. I especially loved the book of John with its emphasis on divine love, *agape*. The Bible seemed like a living thing. Again and again, it described my experience in the here and now. I was amazed and awestruck by its immediacy.

I confided in Mary about my continuing struggle with celibacy. It was wonderful to share with someone I trusted outside of the monastery. Over my years as a monk, the fight with celibacy had waxed and waned, but long-lasting physical peace seemed unattainable. Sexuality had been a place of suffering long before I became a monk. Now the battle was sharper and more painful than ever. It felt like a high internal divide between two fundamentally opposed forces, both deeply embedded in my own heart. I saw the body and its "needs" as something lower, an internal enemy I must overcome.

Mary knew what I was talking about, but with a crucial difference. For Christians, life is a battleground between God's righteousness and very real forces of evil, intent on counterfeiting

that "rightness" with lies. Unlike my own homegrown, partially-understood conclusions, the Christian's battle is not against his flesh and blood. Christian sexuality, lived within God's framework, is a divine, beautiful manifestation of life. The rulers and authorities of Satan's dark world counterfeited sexuality's power, twisting it into something destructive through the forces of lust, hatred, and ignorance.

Mary recited Ephesians 6:12 (NIV): "For our struggle is not

against flesh and blood, but against the rulers, against the authorities, against the powers of this dark world."

My response to this was anything but intellectual. Immediately upon hearing the passage, I felt a powerful physical punch in the middle of my back. Two bolts of high-voltage energy rippled up and

Goofing around in Alaska with grand-nieces & nephews

down my spine. I burst into tears. It was clear that this battle wasn't about me. I was just another soldier with a need to choose where to stand and fight. If I wanted to follow God's way, I needed to arm myself with faith in His grace and cultivate confidence in my salvation through Christ. Sexuality was something sacred and beautiful under God's plan, not something to repress.

Unlike the Buddhist non-dual worldview, my experience showed me that there was a battle between good and evil in this world — and there was a need to choose sides. So, I moved another step closer to the Christian worldview and away from Buddhism.

As the rest of my family arrived, I met Connie's grandchildren for the first time. What a wonderful, innocent and pure group they were! They got along well together, and kindness was everywhere evident in their interactions.

By the end of the reunion, I was seriously thinking about the real possibility of becoming a Christian. Of course, there were significant obstacles. I was a Buddhist monk! How was I to re-enter the world when I had given up everything, including divesting myself of all my worldly assets? I simply held the issue in my heart as I enjoyed the intimate company of my family during the remainder of the reunion.

My Brother David's son,
Steven

I had been experiencing some breathlessness during the last week of the reunion. I sat quietly and listened to the intense beating of my heart, thumping along at a far faster level than was warranted by my activities. Then, during the flight back to the monastery, I was barely able to walk between gates to board the final leg to Oakland. By the time I reached Oakland, I could not walk at all without beginning to lose consciousness. Barely making it off the plane, I requested a wheelchair at the airport.

At the emergency room, the doctors found that I was suffering from many small blood clots in my lungs. I spent the next eleven days in the hospital. As I lay in the little room, a long line of Christians visited and offered me their testimony. The hospital's chaplain spent hours with me and introduced me to a missionary working in Thailand who was back in California for a few weeks to visit his parents. My sister, Connie, requested that several local clergies visit me. Christian nurses working on the floor testified to me about their faith. It seemed that every day, Christians visited me from somewhere. Also, I spent hours on the phone talking with my family. My only reading material was the modern Bible paraphrase, "The Message."

This was the second life-threatening illness involving blood clots within two years. The doctor assigned to my case made his opinion clear. If I was to continue the sedentary lifestyle of a monk, I risked another clot soon — and this time I could easily die from it. He advised me to stop sitting in the cross-legged meditation posture. He believed that this enhanced the possibility of clots forming in my lower legs. He encouraged me to involve myself in an occupation that allowed more physical movement and to begin a regular exercise regimen to reach aerobic fitness. He also proposed a more regular eating schedule. These suggestions were difficult, perhaps even impossible to attain within the confines of the robes.

Sleeping in my hospital bed, I dreamed a powerful dream, repeating it three times. In the dream, there were three beings, a sea lion, an elephant and an amorphous bag that looked something like a leech distended with blood. The leech-like, shape-shifting bag violently attacked and swallowed the peaceful and refined elephant, which put up no struggle. The sea lion intervened, but seemed very polite, at first helping the elephant resist the leech-like shape-shifting form, but then desisting, seemingly at ease with the violence taking place.

The elephant is an Asian symbol for Buddhist wisdom. The amorphous animal exuded violence and evil. I had seen the world like this, shapeless cancer, all hopes and dreams pulled into the death-like maw of the flesh. To some to whom I described the dream, the polite sea lion seemed to represent a Christ-like nature.

Another time I dreamed that I was in the presence of two human-like beings standing on either side of my hospital bed, each holding the handle of a broadsword, tips resting on the floor between their feet. Perhaps they were angels. I didn't know. Regardless, I wasn't sure whether these "guardians" were protectors or jailers!

One evening I felt a new brokenness. Speaking with my brother over the phone, I crouched on my knees on the floor beside my bed. I felt as if I was lying in an incubator. I had read Paul's great words about how God's power is made perfect in our weakness. Bathed in sweat, I told John that I had never felt so broken, that my heart felt like it was in a thousand tiny pieces. He asked if I wished to place my trust in Jesus. I said I did. We prayed a simple prayer together.

I resolved to leave the robes and re-enter the world as a Christian. I certainly did not completely understand Christianity, but I knew that I could choose Jesus.

So I did. His presence had an undeniable stamp of realness. He and I: it was a relationship both powerful and intimate, a feeling of complete and non-judgmental love, of easy forgiveness. It was undeniable. I was His child, He my deepest friend and real Father.

Through those 40 years of rebellion, God had never left me. Always a complete gentleman, the Holy Spirit had waited until I broke enough to turn to Him. The moment I had made a slight movement in His direction, He was there, present. I had lived the life of the unforgiven, while all the time forgiveness had been available just by turning to its source, Jesus Christ.

I formally disrobed about ten days after returning to the monastery, after training others in the roles to which I had been entrusted.

11

Relationship

Resting in Jesus and His word was my new home. Paraphrasing T.S. Elliot, it felt like I was living in a state of utter simplicity, a state that had cost nothing less than everything.

I left the monastery with nothing but a set of clothes bought at Walmart by William, a lay friend who had just left his postulant status at the monastery. Brother John had mailed me a plane ticket to bring me to his home in Memphis. It felt very odd, leaving the monastery with "civilian" clothes. William and I stopped for a break at a Starbucks halfway through our two-hour ride south to the San Francisco airport. I bought a bottle of water, handing money I had not touched for five years to the bored cashier. We drove on, and I boarded the flight and entered the vast anonymity of this new world order, America.

While I still carried some of the sensibilities of a middle-class professional, I was also undeniably homeless and penniless. I brought only a tiny day pack as luggage. As I looked around at the other people up and down the aisles of the Boeing 757, I wondered how I would find a life among these worthy people.

John and Janet's
fancy cocoon

I arrived in Memphis. My brother and his wife, Janet, lived in suburban air-conditioned comfort in a five bedroom, five bath home in an exclusive community half an hour from the center of Memphis. It was a huge home, immaculate throughout with carefully organized, plush furnishings of the highest quality. I couldn't imagine a world farther removed from the moment to moment strength of ascetic life! It was like living in a gift-wrapped cocoon. Everything that assaulted the senses with their immediacy in a life outdoors — temperature, light, sound — were muffled, restrained, buffered.

I remembered experiencing the stark contrast in my life as a meditation practitioner between the air-conditioned sense deprivation of the Massachusetts retreat center and the raw immediacy of unadorned life in an Asian jungle. One insisted on quiet and safety to develop concentrated focus; the other insisted on developing equanimity, patience, and perseverance amidst the raucous howl of jungle life. Both were essential parts of the practice. Meanwhile, in Memphis, I slept on a floor at the foot of a bed in a bedroom each night with a book under my head, disoriented by the plush floating world of the mattress hulking nearby.

Of course, I had no idea what was going to happen next. I read and walked around the subdivision for an hour each morning at dawn, slowly building up my strength in the cool Tennessee mornings. Pat, the widow of eldest brother Dave, brought a van full of his now unneeded clothes and offered them to me to use. They fit perfectly. She also offered me Dave's old laptop computer. John and Janet bought undergarments, shoes, a watch, and other essential things I needed to live in the world.

While John was off to his work as an industrial engineer at International Paper Corp., I spent hours with Janet, reading Christian books aloud, making flashcards affirming who I was in Christ, and even writing out phrases 100 times! Janet saw me as a blank slate, and I was her student. She worked to fill me with Christian basics about how to live each day for the Lord. She started me on a path focused on reading the Bible and prayer. Much of her teachings were helpful to me, and usually, I listened in appreciative silence. A month after arriving in Memphis, a white-robed deacon baptized me before John and Janet's congregation as a new believer in Christ.

But in my reflective meditations, I could not see a future in these present circumstances. Connie and Mary and her husband, Henry, had invited me to Fairbanks, Alaska, offering use of Henry's old farmhouse which stood empty, and I accepted their offer. After about six weeks with John and Janet, I gratefully hugged them goodbye and set out for Alaska.

The mid-September day I arrived, Connie, Connie's daughter Diane, Mary and her husband, Henry, picked me up at the little airport, its runway adjacent to a rectangular lake for floatplanes. In preparation for my arrival, many people had been looking for a car for my use, but nothing had seemed appropriate. On the way to the farm from the airport, a car was parked by the side of the road with a for sale sign in its window. We called the number and found the owner was asking exactly the amount I could spend. We purchased it then and there with Henry covering the immediate cost. At the airport, my niece Diane had mentioned a teaching job that was available at her school. That day I called the principal of the school, interviewed with her the following day and began work there the day after.

I had arrived in Alaska without possessions or direction in life other than that I wanted to live as a Christian. Within a week came all the necessities I needed, including a warm circle of family and friends, a church, a house, a job, and a car! It seemed like my family held me firm, my feet dangling, as necessities resolved themselves. I thanked God every day for my loving family.

The farm house was a Sears and Roebuck kit brought up the new Alcan Highway on a flatbed in the 1940s and placed on Henry's original homestead just over the hill from Fairbanks on a humpy road to Chena Hot Springs. Each joist and stud in the house had a stamped number, ready for its careful reassembly. After sixty Alaskan winters, it was still sturdy, although leaky windows swayed the curtains in the bathroom and I could poke holes in the flue of the old heater in the basement.

The house had been empty for years after Henry and Mary moved to a new home up the slope to the north a half mile. The place was in primary disarray. Construction on a second story of the farmhouse had abruptly halted when Henry's first wife, Pat, had died of cancer 17 years before. The tools still lay on the plywood second floor where they had been put down those many years before. That family had five children crammed into the

The view south from the
living room picture window

little house, most sleeping in the basement. They lived hard lives growing up in Alaska's dramatic 120 degree seasonal swings and the unremitting labor of year-round potato farming.

The structure was at the center of a large deep-grass meadow filled with all sorts of heavy machinery, buses, dump trucks, old cars, shipping containers, earth movers, all interspersed with a myriad of supplies and miscellaneous junk. Henry was a packrat and an auction addict. He had collected enormous quantities of everything imaginable. As a survivor of many harsh years farming first potatoes, and after his first wife had died, growing hay, he believed it all was essential. It was true that if something broke, he could quickly cobble something together with what was on hand and within easy arms reach. And he knew where everything was until his last half dozen years, when his Alzheimer's disease began its inevitable devolution about the same time I arrived.

Beyond the junkyard was a 350-acre hay field, vast, green and gently undulating. South from there, the land dropped off, and it seemed the world stretched away into infinity. Out the front window of the farm house, one saw an incredible view of the Alaska and Wrangell — Saint Elias Ranges, all spread out edge to edge 120 miles away across the tundra. On clear days one could see the big ice cream scoop of Mt. McKinley further west.

I painted all the walls and organized the chaos of abandoned things inside the house. In nooks and crannies all over the place, I found discarded odds and ends that I slowly put together to make a comfortable living area, a study, and a sleeping area. In short order, it had my personal stamp, and everything I needed to live a simple life was available. I was no longer homeless.

Content

If there is something
To take when I go,
I pray it be knowing
How to be content.

Here in this aging body,
With its aching wants,
Fearful chaos in
Delusion's chartless seas.

But walking towards death and beyond,
This clay shape seems to support
This good heart just fine.

The new job started immediately. Suddenly I was responsible for supervising 17 third graders in a 250-student private Christian school teaching grades K through 12. The old teacher had walked out in a huff three weeks before my arrival, and the Chief Administrator was frantic to find a replacement. Sister Connie had taught there 15 years before and had left positive memories, and my niece was the present administrative secretary. Concerns about my Buddhist past were effectively dispelled through a few hours of conversation and a visit with the Board of Directors.

I didn't know what hit me. That first evening after school I could do no more than lie on the floor of the farmhouse with my arms flung out, utterly exhausted. What had I gotten myself into?

Anyone who has children can understand the chaos made by 17 eight-year-olds facing a neophyte teacher who had never had children of his own. Many of the kids were children of Stryker battalion soldiers stationed at the nearby Army base. A few were brilliant, and a few were slow, but they all liked to have fun. I

Third graders in Mr. VanLeit's
third grade class

struggled hard to speed up to meet my whirling instructional task!

Each morning, after a 20-minute devotional study among the teachers, I herded my group of cats to an assembly where we sang simple Christian songs and heard a wide variety of short, inspirational talks. Each Friday, each class stood and recited the Bible passage they had memorized that week. There was much merriment one Friday when the 6th graders got to choose their passage instead of having it assigned by their instructor. Smiling to a kid, they dramatically recited, "Jesus wept." Everyone enthusiastically approved. It had been the same every year.

I followed a Christian instructional guide based on worksheets and readers, and through this format I taught math, reading, science, geography and social studies. Yes, there was an occasional temper tantrum, and one unusually precocious little girl could vomit on demand if she didn't get her way, but overall the year unfolded well. The administrator was pleased with my work, and with one or two exceptions, the parents accepted me and approved with what I was doing with their child. I couldn't stand the interminable faculty meetings, and each Wednesday I searched diligently for an excuse and snuck out early.

Meanwhile, the Alaskan winter unfolded. The first snow flew shortly after my school year began in mid-September, and it stayed

Outside the kitchen window at the farmhouse.

on the ground until late April. Fairbanks is in the center of the state, four hours south of the Arctic Circle, on high rolling loess soils, soils carried in the air over the centuries from the Siberian vastness far away west across the Bering Sea. There are only 10 or 11 inches of rain each year, so once the freeze started in the fall, the roads quickly cleared and dried while a moderate snowpack covered everything else.

As fall flashed by and the long arctic winter unfolded, darkness increasingly enveloped the landscape. The sun slowly rose at an extreme angle, followed just above the horizon from east to west, and then as if exhausted, sank back below the horizon by mid-afternoon. The light was tremulous and weak. By mid-December, a dim half-light dawn would creep in around 9 a.m. and fade away by 3 p.m. Average temperatures plunged to 20 below zero. If it was above that mark, the kids could bundle up in snowmobile suits, hats, and thick mittens and play in the snow outdoors for half an hour.

Teaching filled time during the weekdays. In the evenings, I would slowly walk back and forth in the main room of the farmhouse listening to Christian music from the laptop. Early each morning, I spent 40 minutes reading the Bible on the phone to Janet's elderly mother in faraway Florida. We read through the whole book and half way again that way. Weekends I would go out with one of my sisters or relax and read. I had a small group from church that met weekly, and we shared our various problems together as well. My life was relatively settled, and I was content.

Despite my history of wandering, I loved family and its attendant domesticity, and it was the desire of my heart to be in a relationship again. Contacting Joan, we spoke about our lives and futures, and it became apparent to both of us that our paths had diverged. There was no going back there.

Looking towards town
from the farmhouse

I also began to yearn to have children. When I was younger, when most young men had become fathers, I had grave fears that the trauma of my years as a child with Ted would cause additional suffering. I knew that there was a statistical tendency to pass on such trauma from generation to generation, and I wanted nothing to do with creating such suffering in the world. But now I was confident that there was no such "predatory virus" that would prevent me from being a father and enjoying children. But I also knew that I was older than most fathers and that it was likely that I could never fulfill this dream.

As the weeks of Alaska's dark, deep-freeze winter progressed, I became increasingly lonely. I wanted to share my life more intimately than the present circumstances permitted. I told Connie it felt like camping out in one small room in the big house that was me. I needed a mate to help me turn on the lights.

I eventually met Katie online, a worship leader in a midsize non-denominational church in a small town in Indiana. She was bright and a marvelous conversationalist. Our long-distance conversations lifted my spirits considerably, and as our relationship developed, I began to think that she could be "the one."

That spring, she visited me. We deepened our relationship by spending a week together, she spending the nights at Mary's house up the hill from the farmhouse. We visited Denali National Park together and wandered around central Alaska. I thought

Croquet with the kids

Holding up the planet at
the Arctic Circle

this was love. Katie had three young adult children, and their personalities and unfolding dreams added flavor to our relationship.

As the school year ended, I began working as a tour guide driving northern Alaska. I would drive a small busload of perhaps 25 visitors up to the Arctic Circle and back (an 18-hour round trip) or drive a smaller group up the Trans-Alaskan Pipeline Highway to Coldfoot, the Brooks Range or even beyond to the oil fields at Prudhoe Bay and the Arctic Ocean.

It was great fun. The summer weather and the constant interaction with interesting people gave me much pleasure. I studied a two-inch-thick binder, a proprietary compendium of all the local color and fascinating histories of the regions we would travel through, and I memorized much of its contents. During tours, I talked for hours about the history, culture, geography, and technologies that were part of the northern Alaska landscape and its peoples.

After a visit to Indiana and a second visit by Katie to Alaska, it was becoming clear that this was serious. I proposed marriage. The obvious problem was that we both had established lives thousands of miles apart. I could see continuing my teaching and summer work as a guide into the foreseeable future. Both were challenging, satisfying occupations. But both did not pay much and neither offered any likely way to advance to higher salaries. If I remained there,

I could support myself, but I would always be on edge financially, dependent on my sister for free rent and an outlying satellite in family activities. I would be the lonely bachelor uncle who was always welcomed, but largely peripheral.

Travelling through the Brooks Range to the Arctic Ocean

On the other hand, I knew nothing about life in Katie's small Indiana town. I was still licensed to practice law in New Mexico, but there was no reciprocity with Indiana. I would have to start over by studying and then taking the state's bar exam. Small town life could be ingrown, and I feared that it would be difficult for me to find work there.

Still, without a direct yes or no to my proposal of marriage, I left Alaska and moved to Ohio, setting up housekeeping in the empty home of a local dentist's deceased mother a few minutes away from Katie's house. Brother John offered me an older mini-van that he no longer needed. I sold my little car and kissed my sisters goodbye and flew south.

Indiana was a shock. It felt alien, and while I looked for work everywhere, there was simply nothing to be had. Katie agreed to marry me on Valentine's Day, but on the advice of her best friend, backed out only a few weeks later. They thought I was just too risky. I was jobless, and with my hard-to-explain history, my future seemed iffy. My small savings vanishing, my relationship with Katie foundered. Finally, I left Indiana and my hopes for a future with Katie. I headed to Memphis and John and Janet, penniless and discouraged. I arrived on April Fool's Day, 2008.

12

God Makes the World for Me

t didn't take a rocket scientist to figure out that my wrenching sadness, sense of defeat and zeroed out pocketbook were the results of some fundamentally wrong thinking. I had been sure that Katie was "the one" and had bet everything that it would turn out right. But my experiences in Indiana showed me that I was just as good at deluding myself after practicing as a monk all those years as I had been before. While I was committed to our future together, I had not noticed that she was genuinely confused about her motivations.

I also began to realize that I had gotten something fundamentally wrong in my new relationship with Christ. The early success I had in re-entering the world had made it easy to hold to that idea that somehow if I did it right, He would always bless me. That was the way I figured it when I was a little boy, and now it was the way I was thinking about it still!

I borrowed money from John and moved into one of their five bedrooms. I felt terribly alone. John and Janet did everything they could to cheer me up, but I could not lift my head for months. Still, I started looking around town for work. My prior work experiences had been in Alaska and a tiny town in the Midwest, both isolated and not growing economically, so I reasoned that Memphis with its much larger economic base would make it easier to find work.

I was wrong. There seemed to be significant barriers in front of every effort I made. Just a few months after my arrival, the national economy took a huge nosedive, losing almost a quarter of its value in a few months. Professional opportunities appeared unavailable. I needed to go back to college for several years to become a licensed Tennessee teacher, and I had neither the youth nor the financial resources to make that work. With or without a teaching license, I had no Christian track record to convince private Christian schools that I would be a good choice. My law license was from another state that had no reciprocity with Tennessee. And for other businesses in town, I was an older, over-qualified applicant with a largely unexplainable hole in my resume. I applied everywhere but got nowhere. Even working at the FedEx hub throwing boxes at night was nixed after they learned that I had not been living in the U.S. for the last five years. According to rules from Homeland Security, that made me a security risk.

Of course, Brother John knew my history as a successful professional. He was sure that I could build on my greatest strength — my experience as an attorney. I felt no joy in the prospect, but after months of failure, I was ready to try anything. I bought a used set of bar exam study materials and began the inglorious task of outlining a dozen major areas of Tennessee law in preparation for the bar exam.

Meanwhile, I took a one week course and became licensed as an insurance agent. I began work on commission with an apparently successful life insurance company. Several months later, after not making a single sale, I gave that up too. That misguided adventure just made things worse.

One bright area in my life was a small group of men that I met every Saturday morning down at the Perkins Restaurant. They each had their unique stories, and while all were much more stable financially than I, I saw and empathized with the multitude of ongoing struggles each faced. I was not alone. They reminded me that even in my precarious circumstances, being close to Christ made it so much easier. Still a mess, I was a forgiven mess.

One Saturday morning I was talking about my continuing employment difficulties, and one of the men offered me a job. He was apologetic, but he said that if I wanted just anything, he could get me a job at Burger King. I quickly said yes, and after one phone call, I was employed.

In the depths of the financial meltdown now called the "Great Recession," the only work this aging white guy could find was taking orders at the neighborhood Burger King, and I got that job only because I knew the manager from church! Nevertheless, I was grateful and blessed for this daily exercise in humility. It was work, and so I enjoyed it. I worked there for almost a year.

I must say that I was bad at being a Burger King counter person, or "expedited cuisine delivery agent." The work went on at a breakneck pace, and I continually bungled the complex procedures, but I slowly learned the ropes to the point where I was at least minimally competent. It was challenging work, both because I was on my feet for hours at a time and because the pace was very fast. I've always loved to work hard, and here I worked hard every day, coming home bone tired at night and sleeping well.

For all this, I got one dollar above minimum wage, $7.50 an hour, and then sworn to secrecy so my grand pay scale would not generate jealousy amongst the other workers. There were no benefits, and one could be fired anytime at the whim of a shift manager. One worked just under forty hours a week to avoid any possibility of overtime. After everything was taken out at the end of the week, I could now pay for gas, as well as an occasional piece of clothing or other personal item, but there was little hope that I could save up to buy a car or rent a small apartment.

Most of the other workers received government assistance to remain economically viable. Even though they worked very hard at a mostly thankless job, they were not going to make it without help from the state. They were real people, trapped in poverty without diplomas and with little hope for the future. It was only the circumstances of my birth and the grace of God that allowed me to return home across town to the beautiful subdivision where my brother lived.

I was comfortable, yes, and my brother would never allow me to starve. But I was just a burger flipper making minimum wage and living off the generosity of relatives, and there did not seem to be anything I could do about it. To my old self, I was the classic description of "a failure." What a harsh taskmaster, pride!

Through all that had gone before, I had never let go of a core pride — the pride I had felt as an outstanding student, as a success-ful professional, as an exceptionally ascetic monk and then as a new Christian with an "interesting" story. Now I had to humble myself in a new way.

My routine was simple: I worked, I read, I studied for the bar. I read the Bible daily with John and Janet. Life slowly stabilized, and I came to accept my new circumstances — and my lowly status. One day I was out mowing the lawn when a neighbor across the street came over to talk. When I explained that I was helping my brother, he said, "So you're his yard boy, aren't you?"

He was right, and I felt a simple acquiescence to his intended slur. It was all OK. I had a peaceful and quiet heart. I had enough, and God was good. There was no need to lean into the future and plan. I had tried that with no success. It was OK right where it was right now. I rested.

And that's when things changed. I met a lovely, sensitive woman named Cathy at Sunday school. Self-possessed and dignified, it was clear that she had known sorrow and failure. She had a profound and simple humility and a deeply spiritual sensibility. She was beautiful. I was introduced to her and told her I worked at Burger King, and amazingly, she did not seem to mind.

Around the same time, in conversation with a teacher friend I had met at Sunday school, I was told of the existence of a new program designed to allow professionals the opportunity to teach in the city school system while obtaining professional teaching licensure. I applied, and wonder of wonders was accepted into the Memphis Teaching Fellows program.

The program fit my needs perfectly. The deal was this: I would go through a brief introductory training, commit to teaching for at least three years in Special Education and complete 30 hours of college coursework over the next three years, and thereby earn full licensure. I happily agreed and made the necessary commitments. I participated in half a dozen training sessions capped by six weeks of practice teaching, and in the fall, I began teaching in a city school as an "alternatively licensed" teacher.

Like the Alaskan adventure, my life swung again from somnolence to accelerated evolution. In February 2009, I met the person who became the love of my life. In June, I began to train for a new professional career as a teacher. In July, I married that gloriously southern woman, born in Louisiana and raised in the south, and finally, in August, I began to teach children with disabilities in a classroom every day. The same month I moved to an enormous house located in a distant suburb with my wife and her parents and started to get to know two new "step" children, now young adults.

This new life seemed to burst fully formed from the forehead of God. First came a revolution in Christ, then marriage, then profession. I was just getting by living a lonely life with my brother. Now — suddenly — I was thrust into the center of things in Memphis.

13

Contentment in Constant Revolution

Right from the start, the will of God sends us in directions largely outside our control. Born in a particular place and time, we are at once presented with specific needs requiring an immediate response. The body rages for food and demands maintenance, the mind ceaselessly scans the environment and lusts for information, while the heart seeks desperately for vision, purpose, and direction.

Out of this God-made "ooze" comes the miraculous shape of our lives. Each vector that pushes us is met by some countervailing personal force, something that rises from our core, pushing back. At first, unburdened by self-control or awareness, we just react. But over time, action and reaction are observed, and an awareness of joined result or synthesis emerges.

There is no final synthesis other than death and immortality itself. One moment's synthesis is the action of the next moment, itself generating consequences and new mergers. And so, cobbled together from a welter of these actions and responses, a path opens ahead, and we walk it.

This road of mine leads through many worlds! From the time of my departure from the church in adolescence, I chose the edge of things — first as an eco-warrior and tree planter, then a liberal arts student. As a lawyer, I headed to the edge, immersing myself in public interest work representing juveniles, far from the legal mainstream. Certainly, the Buddhist path to the monastic life would be a "fringe" activity! So too, as a new Christian, I had first sought out the wilds of Alaska within which to root.

Now it looked like circumstances had impelled me toward the very center of the America's conservative cultural mainstream. I committed my heart and soul to locating in this mysterious new foreign place, Memphis, the "buckle of the Bible Belt."

After Jesus, Cathy utterly transformed me. Again and again, I luxuriated in a cascade of blessings coming from her. She seemed the personification of God's grace, unearned, unmerited, vital and complete. She was beautiful, smart as a whip, dignified, sober-minded, focused, modest and humble, professional and articulate, tender hearted, sweet and on top of all that strength, vulnerable! The dominant feeling that pervaded me during our early times together was a sense of honor at being in her presence. She exhibited a quintessential self-possession, at ease yet alert, critically minded but compassionate, sensitive to the experience of life.

We had first met in February of 2009 at a potluck sponsored by our fellowship group from church. We spent the whole evening talking, and the next week I invited her to a nearby café for coffee. We identified as fellow travelers, intimate with each other's spiritual lives like we were brother and sister meeting for the first time. At one point, I screwed up my courage and asked her if I could hold her hand.

"Oh boy," she said! We met for coffee every evening after work those next weeks, spending almost all our free time together. She asked brother John about my trustworthiness. With great earnestness, he told her that he would trust me with his life. I suggested that she call and talk to my former wife, and she did, apparently getting a good report. I proposed marriage a month later, and she quietly and directly agreed.

We married in a simple church ceremony four months later. Both of us were scarred by what had come before, as most older people are. But we came to our new union with a focused vision — that our union was to be God-centered, indivisible and passionate.

Paul teaches that Christian marriage is a microcosm of Christ's relationship with us as humans and with the church. So just as Christ sacrificed everything for His church and us individually, so there were sacrifices to be made in our worldly trinity. Autonomy replaced with interdependency. Personal goals confined to those permanently intertwined with the other. And throughout there is a foundation of spiritual, intellectual, moral, emotional and physical support. Just as a spiritual path with heart centers on a dying to self, so Christian marriage centers on a dying into each other.

I had thought of marriage in years past as a kind of contract agreed between equal partners, but Christian marriage had clearly different roles for man and woman. A Christian husband is to serve and support his mate, loving her through sacrifice. A Christian wife is to trust, respect and support the leadership of her mate. Each actively and consciously gives up self to serve the other.

What seems impossible becomes a reality when Christ is at the center of relationship. Yes, we are both idealists, but both of us submit to God's ultimate authority. Neither leads except through prayer and guidance from the One over all. Neither of us can practice egoism without being shamed by its crudity. So, we break and we each submit to the other, and both of us together to Him.

Although we fail at this regularly, this remains our touchstone to which we return.

Of course, there are disagreements, but over time we have come into the habit of trusting each other, inevitably broken and damaged as we both are. And so, in ways mysterious and unexpected, we each deepen to the other, again and again, and when we thought we could not be any closer, yet again, we deepen. It appears through these old eyes that the crowning achievement of this life is my marriage with my Honey Darlin'.

"Going to church" in Alaska was a simple affair. Bundled up in their many layers, everyone would trudge across the dark, snow-covered parking area towards our meeting place, a hulking windowless box of a building, every surface protected from the wind with a corrugated sheet metal sheath. Inside, water dripped from boots onto the aging red carpet as kids ran around and parents chatted, wreathed in t-shirts and scarves.

Worship music came from a family-based group that included two electricians and the building maintenance man. There was nothing fancy or pretentious going on, just honest and sincere connections with the Lord through music, thoughtful conversation, and an occasional flag waving celebrator. Members of the "audience" regularly joined the worship or came up to witness to the assembly. The differences between staff and congregation were small.

Going to church in Memphis was different. Church attendance is at the center of Memphis culture. It is paved, buttoned up, and wholly mainstream. Now I became acquainted with the rhythms of southern church life. On Sundays, one went to Sunday school first thing in the morning for an hour, then on to the worship service, breaking for dinner and a snooze and thence returning in the evening for a slightly more intimate and perhaps more prayerful service.

Then one went about one's life until Wednesday night. On Wednesday evenings, everyone met to share a meal together, followed by a short worship service and another accompanying homily.

Interspersed among these defined events were more informal gatherings, as well as community Bible studies and daily personal Bible studies. Southern churches have a wide array of courses complete with DVDs and workbooks through which one could join in the study of books of the Bible or a Biblical theme either at home by oneself, as a couple, or in a small group. This Sunday/Wednesday centric cycle defined the weeks and years of southern church life.

I initially joined the church attended by John and his wife, Janet, but here valid membership seemed to require a particular socio-economic status. There was an unspoken exclusivity about the place that made it harder for me to draw close to people. If I appeared too different, I became someone uninteresting to know or befriend. Instead, I was to be prayed over, seeking a future coming forth into respectability, and otherwise ignored.

There is a siege mentality woven into the currents of traditional southern life and the practices of its church. It is a culture on the defensive, wounded and proud. Tellingly, times of church attendance were also the most racially segregated times in our city.

A black friend told me a story from his South Carolina childhood where his black church was located directly across the street — but worlds apart — from the small town's biggest white church. As a teen, he ventured out for the first time beyond the cultural circles of his black church to visit across the street.

Some white parishioners meeting him appeared confused: perhaps he had just lost his place in line and needed some direction.

But the main takeaway that Sunday morning was white disinterest. He was largely ignored — shunned.

What was even more surprising was the response back at his church of origin. Black folks there were universally emotional, angry with him for crossing the divide. He was told in no uncertain terms never to try that again. I imagine they thought of their young man wandering about as if he had visited some lonely shore, foolishly walking among slumbering alligators...

But I came to all this history with a distinctly personal perspective: I wanted to worship my God among other worshipers — any worshipers! I reveled in the centrality of the church in the life of my newly adopted community and spent little time thinking about its dark underside. Instead of sweatshirts in church, I now wore a conservative suit and tie, carrying it so far that when I was sick and couldn't come to church, I still dressed up to watch the service on TV!

As a stranger, nestled in the anonymity of a mega-church, I met Cathy. She had been married to a preacher and knew the culture from the inside out. She saw it as steeped in hypocrisy, an essential but profoundly flawed part of her life. The undercurrents of mainstream culture so apparent to her became increasingly clear to me as well.

One example was the quarterly Saturday when church volunteers descended on the inner city to paint over graffiti or pick up trash, our way of serving the city. Meanwhile, in a city where more people lived below the poverty line than in any other comparable city in America, our church spent four million dollars a year on landscaping!

As my relationship with Cathy deepened, we struck out together to find a growing non-denominational church focused on racial reconciliation. We found Fellowship Memphis, a true hospital for the saved, where we remain now after many years.

History Painted

It's 8 am,
And Sunday again.
The week's celebration is bound to begin,
With bellowing silver bells summoning in
The saints from all corners to come and attend.

The reverend in blue gets centered.
The choir in robes all enter.
The ushers, church mothers, and members all huddle
As close as mentees and mentors.

I take in this scene of fuchsias and greens,
And grays as crisp as metal machines,
My brother and I, we gazing around,
Among other thoughts, if colors had sounded,
A jungle of hues would steady surround the pews that ground
Our beings.

... So we buckle down.

The choir begins the first golden praise,
Our hymnals before us in pouches.
Admiring one, I turn cream colored pages.
My brother looks on and slouches.
The church in unity's dance, while raising their hands,
All swaying as flowers —
My brother and I then exchange a glance...

We'll be here for the next 6 hours.

I cradle my history like a priceless painting,
A tapestry colored, waxing and waning,
With splotches and swatches of intricacies,
Stretching backward a couple of centuries,
Skin colors of several varieties,
Connected.
Divided ethnicities.
Like settled, yet unsolved mysteries —

Colorful. Complex. Complicated.

Black choirs who sang of peace like a river,
Unspeakably met with violence.
The joy of thanksgiving rang boldly of red,
While slaves met in holiest silence.
And shouts of praise all louder than bombs
Though houses of praise were raided with bombs.
Yes, this priceless painting tells truth of stories
That don't — and — won't disappear.
The red of blood shed we cannot un-see.
And sobs we cannot un-hear.

Transfixed in the front of our minds,
Reminders that brilliantly shine,
That we must never,
No matter how tempting,
Attempt to go colorblind.

I imagine my Creator — a precious painter.
An artist who never sleeps.
His spirit in silence, hovering over the canvas of the deep.

And in his keeping, the angels are patiently waiting to
     dance and rejoice.
As He prepares the paintbrush of his voice.
Creating things no other breathing can repeat —
This canvas, heaven and earth, come forth in color
     When He speaks.
The garden sings of fuchsias and greens,
And grays as crisp as metal machines,
Father, Spirit and Son, all gazing around,
Among other thoughts, if colors had sounded,
A jungle of hues would steady surround this
Human being called Adam
He's shaped from the ground.

Our God divine,
Perfectionist in everything he does —
This artist, far from color blind,
Said passionately many times,
About his masterpieces —
"It is good."

... because it was.

Christ cradles the church —
His precious painting.
A tapestry colored, waxing and waning,
With splotches and swatches of intricacies,
All nations and hues of ethnicities.
Each son and daughter may
Come as they please —
No heritage ever diminished.
This painting, this story of us, is perfect

Because of what He has finished.
All nations welcomed, near and far
To unashamedly come as you are,
To give him your heart and
transformed mind,
Enjoying the art of being kind
Of people perfected, repurposed and free.
A body of colors in unity.

We'll be here an eternity.

A vision of beauty sublime.
Once blind, but now we see near and far,
And unashamedly come as we are —
Of this art in us, our God affirms —
"It is good."

Because we are.

By Jazmin "Jazzy" Miller

While teaching in Alaska, I had followed a very precise pre-published daily lesson plan with accompanying worksheets. Every responsibility had been laid out in great detail. I followed the directions and thereby appeared to be a successful teacher while getting barely more income than I had earned at Burger King.

Memphis Teaching Fellows trained me in much more general ways so that I could make daily lesson plans of my own as I went. Such brief training of necessity was cursory and left me with some general ideas but little experience and when I got my first teaching assignment, I was pretty much on my own.

I was assigned to an inner-city elementary school and given a class of children whose disabilities made them unable to be successful in a regular grade leveled class. Ms Jefferson, my assistant, blanketted with tattoos and sporting a gold tooth, held mysterious hours. She would drive off in her Infiniti for no reason, leaving me to guess at her mysterious source of income.

My dozen students came from kindergarten, first, second, third, fourth and fifth grades. They included kids with intellectual disabilities, legal blindness, autism, conduct disorders, intermittent explosive disorders, post-traumatic stress disorders and severe attention deficits. All the kids were officially impoverished and therefore eligible for free breakfast and lunches.

Fortunately, most of the time we were left to our own devices, but I got little in the way of direction or support. Confronted as I was with a very wide range of learning capabilities, I grew increasingly confused as to what it was I should — or could — teach. Some of the rougher kids, sensing my uncertainty, took off on behavioral sprees that took my breath away. Some of these behaviors were really extreme: screaming, hitting heads against walls, breaking windows, fighting, running, kicking over chairs and desks, bolting out the door and running down the halls (or worse, outside) and generally being obstreperous. Motivation to learn seemed feeble to nonexistent. Some days it was all my single assistant and I could do to survive the day without major "incidents."

Against this behavioral backdrop, I tried to teach to the whole group but found it almost impossible to do. I was largely unaware of the larger structure of what children generally should be learning in each course at each of the six grade levels within which I taught. I only realized a month from the end of the year that there were detailed grade-specific teaching outlines for each subject buried three levels down in the school system's central website!

So, I attempted to bore down, giving each student individual work assignments. This was like trying to teach four major subject areas in six grade levels all at once, and that's not even mentioning each child's unique disabilities and how that impinged on what they knew, how they learned it and what teaching strategy would be most effective in reaching them. It was a difficult challenge to pinpoint where each child was and then actually measure and test his or her progress. I eventually came to rely on standardized tests available on the internet to try to guide my teaching and measure student progress. I was consciously putting the cart before the horse, but I didn't know what else to do.

I barely survived that first year of teaching. Later I understood that most new teachers felt the same way I did even if they were teaching only one grade level and had good academic maps. Cathy and my pride kept me afloat.

Meanwhile, there was precious little support from the administration. After about a month in the job, I began to realize that my principal was actively targeting me. Instead of supporting my best efforts with guidance and information, I was being undermined by my supervisor! Regular verbal insults, write-ups on hyper-technical grounds and a complete lack of interest in training me led to a tough relationship. By the end of the year, I saw a pattern: of the five white teachers in the building, all were either fired or quit. I had never been the object of racism before, but the distinct differences in how the principal treated white teachers and black teachers made its impact clear. It was only the first of several examples of how important the attitude of the principal of a school was in defining the culture found there.

At the end of the year, I was placed in a pool of teachers who had no position. After calling another highly trusted teacher known to both of us, a fierce and focused African American principal looked across the table at me during a mass interview day and told me he wanted to hire me. "My friend says that you cared about the kids," he said, "and that's all I need to know."

So, I moved to a starkly different teaching environment. I now shared with another teacher a group of twenty-four exceptional middle school (junior high) students who were deemed unable to succeed in mainstream classes. We split the group into two groups of twelve and switched mid-day. While some exhibited extreme behaviors on occasion, there was immediate support from the principal's office, and such responses ended quickly.

I slowly began to develop strategies that brought into focus what was taught as a group and what needed to be brought down to an individual student's level. Laptop access helped enormously in this, especially in math: here, the diagnostic component was rapid and automatic with immediate feedback after every answer. If a student did not grasp a problem, the software would bring him back to the basics needing to be learned. After the review, the problem would be paraphrased and re-introduced. Often, real progress resulted from this combination of approaches, and I began to experience great satisfaction seeing children learning and enjoying it.

I remained in self-contained special education classrooms during my entire teaching career. The last few years I taught seventeen kindergarten and first-grade autistic kids at an elementary school with three assistants. When I came of retirement age, and after it became apparent that my aging in-laws needed my help, I retired with a small pension. In all, I taught seven years.

Everyone can and does learn given the right environment. I worked hard to make that happen, and I sincerely hope that those efforts bear fruit in the future lives of those I taught.

Since retirement, this body has begun to deteriorate. I've suffered from pulmonary embolisms, a rare kind of pneumonia, and COPD. I now must use supplemental oxygen to remain active.

14

Good-by for Now

Recently, I traveled deep into the heart of Denali National Park with a dozen family members. The valleys and swelling mountain shoulders are vast and beautiful by themselves, but they are dwarfed by the enormity of Mount McKinley, a 20,000-foot giant scoop of ice cream and the largest mountain in North America.

It's not the highest mountain in the world—there are some 140 higher ones. But it has the greatest front range found anywhere, extending up in vast walls of buttress upon buttress, rising shoulder to curling shoulder of rock up some 20,000 feet straight up into the sky from the sea, a sheer wall of ice and rock.

I hadn't been back to Alaska in several years. Cathy and I were both surprised by the hot and sunny weather we found when we arrived. We had brought warmies, but not much in the way of subtropical clothing! But then our clear hot weather disappeared. In its place was a cold, steady rain, and at one point, even snow. Our tour bus was still packed with tourists, eager in anticipation of mountain viewing on a grand scale. But alas, it was not to be. Instead, the mountain itself was hidden from us. We drove for hours in the valley, surrounded by mist, the windows covered with mud spray and fogged with our breath.

So, most of us travel through life, looking at the foothills, inferring the existence of a mountain nearby, but unable to see anything but its base. The misty mountains remain hidden. Some despair of ever seeing it and go about life content to stay in the foothills. Others deny the mountain's existence and argue that only what we can see and touch is real. A few just keep looking, straining to see. And sometimes the clouds part, and sometimes they do see.

I style myself an expert at all these strategies. I've tried to hide in earthly relationships, in careers and general business. I've been an ardent atheist, denying the existence of anything but the observable processes of life. I've been a legalist and a religionist. Now I am a "person of faith," a follower of Jesus. Now, I feel the peace of something akin to knowledge only when I step aside and accept how little I know — and can know.

The truth is that this body and this mind is together a worshiping machine, an exquisite antenna, designed to receive the experience of God. We have no choice in this: we are as humans inherently seekers of union with the One God. Each one of us is worshipping something right now. We are inherently religious.

I remember telling Andrew, Joan's father, a renowned scientist, about this belief of mine. I claimed he viewed the scientific method as a religion. He reacted angrily (in fact, he protested too much). I quickly apologized, but like Galileo, I had to silently say that the truth is the truth. All of us hold on to our idols: power, money, intelligence and our feeble knowledge, good looks, success, and class or racial status. The list goes on and on.

Our preferences, even the warp and woof of our logical processes, are shaped by our intelligence and experiences, our upbringings and our readings, our friends, our nation, our class, and so on. What we see as a "logical" process is, in fact, a list of preferences based on the often subterranean psychological substructures in our world that result from these positions. Our *thinking* minds cannot escape the circumstances of our birth. Accepting this inimitable and usually uncomfortable truth is the first step towards wisdom.

Nonetheless, we humans naturally grasp for truth. The secular rationalists among us choose "ultimate truths" based on logic and personal preference. What is different about this than going down to the mall and picking out a new outfit? I see this as "God shopping." I saw a bumper sticker the other day that said, "In the beginning, man created God," and I think a lot of what is called modern religious experience is just that: each of us creating God in our image.

Those who depend on their minds to understand the universe are doomed to live in a self-referencing circle of delusion. When I was a child, I fed on the mother's milk of religious observances: the Gothic-arched church with its stained-glass windows, the robed and vested minister with his outstretched arms blessing the congregation, the peels of Bach organ fugues pouring out the open door into the world. All these things are of inestimable value and are exquisitely beautiful. But lots of Christians today have relationships with their denomination, church building, worship rituals, Sunday school mates, everything religious but that which is at its center — their Creator God.

These human-created shells are not the deep tissue, the underlying bedrock of the experience of God. Religious rituals satisfy essential needs but do not reach down to the life-changing relationship with God. That requires something more — brokenness and faith.

The fount of all faith is the end of our most pervasive idolatry: thinking we know what's going on. Faith is humility in the face of the immeasurable and the unknowable. Humility means "getting small." A genuine measure of spiritual maturity is a profound sense of humility. Jesus tells us to come to him like little children, innocent and open-hearted. He even describes humans as sheep. Looking around — and in the mirror — it is easy to see why.

There is an excellent little book I read years ago called <u>The Cloud of Unknowing</u>. It contains letters from an elderly anonymous Christian monk living in the 17th century to an equally anonymous younger monk. He describes his process of coming to the experience of God. First, he writes, one must consciously and with great effort place a cloud of unknowing over the world. One must step back from the desires of everyday life that are screaming, "fulfill me!" Purify one's mind, clarify one's heart and bring it to its natural home of innocence and humility. The things that exist to inflate us, to show us as "better than:" these things, discard as garbage!

The book goes on: and while all this effort is well and quietly accomplished, we must turn our eyes upward, up to and through the clouds above us. We must pierce that cloud with a yearning, passionate desire to know and to love, to be known and to be loved by God. And then there is a miracle, an ineffable response. A Presence, something clearly beyond, something other, extends a tendril, a line, a cable, an express train of love and connection, and another indescribably beautiful relationship with God begins.

The active part of this relationship is simple service. It's better to think of oneself less and less, and the needs of others more and more. Faith expresses itself in action, a consuming desire to serve a world filled with predators, victims and predator/victims, each caught in a web of suffering whose sources are rarely encountered, much less examined. First and foremost, the life worth living is a life of service.

Sanctum: The Inner Canyon, Grand Canyon National Perk

The best thing that Buddhism taught me was to shut up and listen. Its penetrating critique of the human condition — that all desire naturally leads to suffering and more desire is very much like what Christ taught. But there the similarity ends. Buddhism empties the meditator through nonaction to emptiness, and ultimately, extinction. Christianity fills those who seek Christ's will with a divine relationship, expressed through fervent prayer, humility, joy, and a pure faith.

Read the Bible daily, pray that God's will be done in your life and remain embedded in a local Christian community. God extended himself into the world at the creation. He permeates and holds up that world with His loving care. He knows every hair on each of our bodies as He does every feather on the wing of a sparrow. The prayers of a righteous human go up with strength and vitality, creating a constantly evolving relationship with the One. I am convinced that forty years of prayers going up from my brothers and sisters played a major role in bringing me to a knowledge of Christ. Prayer supports me now and continues to shape my life.

God extended Himself into the human realm with Jesus, coequal and yet distinct, a person who led, and brings us today towards beauty and truth. He takes an active part in my life. It is a simple fact that when invited with all one's heart, He will be experienced. He will awake in your heart, and you will feel His love wholly and without end. So, serve the world to follow Christ's example, to be an innocent ready to suffer for a guilty world. Here is contentment, completion, and happiness.

If you wish to find out about Jesus, "Ask, and it will be given to you; seek, and you will find; knock, and it will be opened to you. For everyone who asks receives, and the one who seeks finds, and to the one who knocks it will be opened." (Luke 11:9-10)

> "May the Lord bless and keep you;
> the Lord make His face to shine upon you
> and be gracious to you;
> the Lord lift up His countenance upon you,
> and give you peace." (Numbers 6:24-26)

Made in the USA
Columbia, SC
23 February 2023

12872446R00102